THE
Infinite Wisdom
of the
Akashic
Records

THE
Infinite Wisdom
of the
Akashic Records

Lisa Barnett

New Page Books
A division of The Career Press, Inc.
Pompton Plains, N.J.

THE INFINITE WISDOM OF THE AKASHIC RECORDS
EDITED AND TYPESET BY KARA KUMPEL
Cover design by Zoe Shtorm
Printed in the U.S.A.

To order this title, please call toll-free 1-800-CAREER-1 (NJ and Canada: 201-848-0310) to order using VISA or MasterCard, or for further information on books from Career Press.

The Career Press, Inc.
220 West Parkway, Unit 12
Pompton Plains, NJ 07444
www.careerpress.com
www.newpagebooks.com

Library of Congress Cataloging-in-Publication Data
CIP Data Available Upon Request.

I dedicate this book to my wondrous father, Don Colby.
You have been my spiritual inspiration,
lovingly sharing your expansive view of life.
Thank you for your unconditional love
and support on my extraordinary spiritual journey.

Acknowledgments

Great gratitude goes out to the Akashic Lords and the Beings of Light who suggested years ago that I reveal Akashic Record knowledge to the world through a school and books. Your love, guidance, and wisdom have transformed my life.

Acknowledgments also go to:

Meg Bertini, for saying "Yes!" when I asked for your help in putting this teaching together in an understandable and linear way. I could not have started it without you.

Linda Berger, my dear friend and fellow Akashic Record teacher. Thank you for being able to see this work from the place of the student. You have made this information comprehendible and clear for all the readers to come. Your support and love, every day, in so many ways, have opened a floodgate in my heart. I couldn't have completed this without you.

My dear husband, Jesse, who has supported me on my spiritual path from the first day we met. You make it possible for me to expand into the infinite wisdom of the Akashic Record so that I may teach, write, travel, and share this profound work. Your love assists me in everything I do.

My dear children—all four of you: Connor, Lilly, Lucia, and Justin. Thank you for your "soul contracts" with me to be your mom. My heart is overflowing with your love. Your innate wisdom has altered my view of the world so many times, in so many ways. I have been blessed to have four baby Buddhas in my house.

All my students and clients whose questions and desires to change their lives have helped me to bring through much of the information you will read in this book.

I thank my fellow Akashic Record teachers and consultants from the greatest expanse of my heart. I wouldn't have come to this point without all the support, editing, and ideas I have received from you. You keep me moving forward on my Akashic path.

To all my friends I haven't mentioned by name, I thank you and I love you. You are the Light that keeps my candle burning. You are the motivation and support that keeps me strong. Thank you.

Disclaimer

This book is intended to provide accurate and helpful information. However, readers are strongly encouraged to consult with a healthcare professional before using any of the information contained in this book. Neither the author nor the publisher are engaged in rendering medical advice or services. Accordingly, the publisher and author disclaim any liability, loss, damage, or injury caused by the use or application of the contents of this work. NO WARRANTY, EXPRESS OR IMPLIED, IS DELIVERED BY THE AUTHOR OR PUBLISHER WITH RESPECT TO THE CONTENTS OF THIS WORK.

Contents

Foreword

by Dawn Marian, DD

Humanity is at an unprecedented time in its history. As the world population tips past 7 billion, we have challenges that have never been faced before on this planet. Now, perhaps more than ever, a guidebook is needed to find our way. The Akashic Record is just that—a map to consult as humankind unfolds its destiny. Once an esoteric sacred practice hidden from the masses and privy only to those in the highest spiritual orders, it has now become accessible to those who seek its wisdom. Its vast realms of information range from the sacred recordings of the history of the cosmos to the journey of each individual soul, and include universal principles for living a joyful and abundant life.

Lisa Barnett has taken this path of ancient wisdom and delivered a straightforward process to access the Akashic Record for modern times. Though simple, it is no less profound than when taught by the mystery schools of yore. The Akashic Record contains solutions to every problem humans face, from a global scale to the everyday challenges of raising families, dealing with health problems, and living a purpose-driven life. It dissolves barriers to abundance, enhances creative expression, and heals emotional wounds. It is a must for anyone who desires to become a living expression of the Light and Love that he or she inherently is, and has always been.

This book is for all seekers of a deeper significance to life. It provides tools to create an authentic life experience based on the expansive intelligence of the soul and the unconditional Love that flows through the Universe. Lisa Barnett succinctly teaches how to easily open the doors of the Akashic Records to those who feel the heart's call to receive the wisdom and healing of the Akashic Field.

It is with whole-hearted admiration and great excitement that I recommend this book, so lovingly written by Lisa Barnett.

Dawn Marian, DD

Akashic Records Teacher

Reiki Master Teacher

Founder of **The Radiant Heart School of Transformation**

Introduction

Do you sometimes feel as though you're playing whack-a-mole with your problems? Do you solve one life issue, only to have another pop up somewhere else? Did you finally get a handle on your money issues, and then suddenly your relationship fell apart? Did you finally lose that unwanted weight with your new exercise program, only to be told you had a heart condition and you needed to stop exercising? Did you manifest your perfect job, and then your life partner found out his or her company was relocating to another state?

Wouldn't it be nice to have a clear, quick, and easy way to resolve the issues that life inevitably throws in your direction? A way that considers all of the influences involved in these situations, including your childhood programming, your ancestral genetics, *and* your past lives? Imagine what it would be like if you could finally have everything you need to know. This is the gift of working in the Akashic Records. And the best part is that you can be filled with unconditional love while you're working through any and all of your issues.

So, what *are* the Akashic Records?

The Akashic Records are records of every soul's journey, from the time it first individuates from Source until it finally returns home—a journey that can take millennia. No matter how new or ancient a soul you are, your Akashic Record holds all your thoughts, feelings, actions, and deeds from each lifetime. You can imagine the Akashic Records as a library, with each book representing a lifetime, or as a computer, with all your information stored on the hard drive. The Akashic Field is part of and connected to the All. It is the information arm of Source. You have your own Masters, Teachers, and Beings of Light that keep track of this information, just for you. You can access these Masters and Teachers, and they will answer your personal questions about this life and lives past that are affecting you today.

The answers to your questions are waiting to be revealed to you, including everything you've ever wanted to know about yourself, whether in your current life or in your past lives. Not only does your Akashic Record contain the answers to your current concerns, but the Record is also ready, willing, and able to assist you in releasing energy blocks that may be preventing you from living a life of fulfillment and abundance. The Akashic Records provide profound, divine wisdom, given with clarity and unconditional love, to help guide you through your day, directing you to and on your soul's path. The wisdom in the Records clears karma and releases negative energy patterns that no longer serve you—negative energy patterns that contribute to financial hardships, create relationship problems, cause unnecessary emotional suffering, and so much more.

The Akashic Records are easy to access, and can assist you in understanding your soul's path. The Beings of Light want to help you. They give this gift to humanity because they feel that by understanding the uniqueness of our soul's path, we will move through our karma to embrace the love that each and every soul is here on earth to experience. Opening the Akashic Records will allow you to begin to realize how soul contracts function, how they're utilized to prepare you for your soul's path, and how they influence your daily choices. It will show you how to work with those contracts for the benefit of increasing love, happiness, and success in your life.

Your Akashic Record can also aid you in identifying and understanding past-life vows, which will affect you in this lifetime until you renounce their necessity and release them. How often have you felt like you've hit a brick wall in your ability to make money? Have you ever experienced the excitement of making a lot of money only to once again return to a state of "just getting by"? This may be because you have an unidentified past-life vow with poverty. For example, my clients often tell me they don't feel that they deserve to charge a fee and make money from the healing work they do. When we go into their personal Akashic Record we see past lives in which they were monks, nuns, or ascetics who took vows of poverty. When you work in the Akashic Records, you can ask your Beings of Light to help you grow and learn from those experiences and to release what no longer serves your life today.

Or maybe you feel as though you've been too controlling in some areas of your life. Perhaps you lived a life or numerous past lives when you vowed to never relinquish your power again. You could have been in government—a ruler who had his or her power taken away during a rebellion or revolt—so in this present life you feel afraid of losing control. The Records can help you release these old energies so they no longer manifest in destructive ways in different parts of your life.

The Akashic Records, although simple to access, are a powerful, profound tool that you can rely on each day in order to make your life easier. The Akashic Records can guide your choices, from the most ordinary, everyday things such as which foods to eat to ensure a healthy body, to how to maximize your efforts to achieve your goals. They can also tell you what could be an underlying cause of an illness and even how you may be able to heal it as you release the core beliefs underlying it. One of my favorite ways to use the Akashic Records is to simply open it and ask your Beings of Light, Teachers, and Lords to put you in God's arms, so that you may experience the pureness of your connection with divinity and its source of brilliant light and unconditional love.

This is only a sampling of what awaits you in your Akashic Record. Like intuition on steroids, the Akashic Records will inspire you, motivate you, and fill your life with grace in a way you've only dreamed is possible. The unconditional love that emanates from the Records is expressed with meaning, caring, and loving kindness.

The Infinite Wisdom of the Akashic Records is filled with powerful processes and prayers to help you access your own Akashic Record and lovingly heal yourself with the help of the Beings of Light, Masters, and Teachers who will guide you every step of the way. It is designed to guide you, step by step, through discovering the following:

1. Vibrational keys (sacred prayers) to simply, directly, and easily access your Akashic Record

2. Important guidelines that hold you in the light of protective love in the Akasha's sacred field of energy

3. The art of formulating questions in order to receive life-enhancing answers

4. How to release negative karma, which binds you to negative life patterns

5. How to access inner wisdom for clarity in order to navigate your life with more precision

6. How to practice accessing your Akashic Record to ensure continued success in receiving more information

7. Additional tools and prayers to assist you in further healing

You are honored, loved, and revered for your great courage in choosing to incarnate in this dimension. The Akashic Records' Beings of Light, Masters, and Teachers wish to serve you so that you may feel blessed in each step that you take toward living your true purpose.

The Infinite Wisdom of the Akashic Records has been written to facilitate great change in the world, one soul at a time, and you are first up. You are going to have the opportunity to clear fears and unnecessary karma so that you can move on to living the life your heart and soul desire. How do you think you found this book? You have already been guided. Your inner being knows of your deep desire to heal and move into the direction of your life purpose. This is a giant step in your path to healing, and I feel blessed that you are allowing me to share this sacred work with you. Thank you for letting me be your teacher by reading *The Infinite Wisdom of the Akashic Records*.

If you are ready to experience unconditional love and feel the radiant light the Akashic Records hold for humanity, it's time to create the life your soul planned before you came here; to live the life you deserve.

I send you blessings on your journey.

Chapter 1

The Library of Your Soul

Akashic Records Basics

The greatest storehouse of infinite knowledge you will ever explore awaits you here! Chapter by chapter you will gain greater understanding of the Akashic Records and the wisdom they can offer you today. You will learn how to open your own Akashic Record, and how to listen for the answers that can untangle your issues, creating forward movement, unencumbered, with ease and with unconditional love.

For now, though, let's start by saying the Akashic Records are the informational arm of Divine Source energy. Those who study the Records often refer to them as a library. They are the Divine library, where, throughout time, soul records of everyone and everything that has a soul have been stored. Every person has his or her own Akashic Record, containing each individual soul's journey throughout time.

Imagine that you have a personal library filled with books and each book represents a lifetime. You may have 600 or 800 lifetimes just here on planet Earth, as well as other planes of existence, other dimensions, other planets, and the angelic and elemental realms, just to name a few. Everything that our souls have thought, felt, or acted upon throughout time is in the Akashic Records. We are infinite beings with vast Akashic Records.

Not only do we, as individuals, have Akashic Records, but our businesses have them as well. As you learn to access your own Record more and more deeply, you can also access the Akashic Record of your business to find many ways to help grow it, including how to best serve your employees and clients. You can also ask the Akashic Records to assist you in finding ways in which your business can be of assistance to humanity. Your family of origin has a group Record that is helpful in working through group dynamics, learning about group contracts, and finding your soul family members in your human family now. For pet owners, you will be happy to know that your pets have an Akashic Record too. You may find it interesting to ask in your own Akashic Record about the past lives you and your pet have shared, and how you can be supportive to them in this life.

All of this information is accessible, but the first step is to learn to enter your own Akashic Record. Do you remember how you first learned to read when you were in first or second grade? And then how you continued to strengthen your reading skills and gained new knowledge by exploring different subjects? That is how it will work for you with the Akashic Records. Once you start learning how to access your own Akashic Record, you'll then continue to grow and explore the Akashic Field each and every time you open your Record. The amount of information in the Akashic Field is infinite in the truest sense of the word, so there is always so much more to experience.

The Akashic Records allow us to see the world from a much different perspective than most humans do—one that is broader and deeper in scope than many humans allow themselves to delve. The image that the Beings of Light have shared shows most of us walking through our daily lives down on street level, just dealing with our issues, traumas, and problems. It is so easy for us, as humans, to get caught up in our daily dramas and the dense energies of this earthly plane. But when we begin to access our own Akashic Record, we are lifted energetically into a very different place on a much higher vibrational plane. It's like being in an airplane looking down on the Earth, where all of the troubles, issues, and traumas appear so much smaller. At that perspective, it is easier for you to see where they all connect, and why you had chosen certain issues to work through in this lifetime. This higher viewpoint offers you a different way of looking at life: instead of seeing it as filled with problems, you are suddenly aware of the opportunities for growth and limitless possibilities your choices have offered you. For example, a person with whom you are in conflict over a business deal might be a piece of the karmic circle you've come here to complete. In your Akashic Record, you start to learn about the connections dating back through time and space from another lifetime. You then realize that the two of you had a similar issue in a past life, and that you have both chosen to finish the karma by working through a business deal this time around with integrity instead of an attitude of "take the money and run," which you may have done in one or more past lives. In this present life, you can choose to be helpful and supportive to that person in order to create a strong business relationship by being the forgiveness you may need to offer and she may need to have you mirror back to her.

By accessing the Akashic Records, we start to see our lives (which often include trauma and emotional pain) in a different way, from a more complete perspective. Before accessing the Records, it was as though we were stuck in a maze, just wandering around hoping to find the exit. The appearance of being in a maze is part of the game our soul chooses to play with us. The only problem is, we don't know it's a game, and we are not aware of the point of playing the game. As we access the Akashic Records, we learn that we are here to remember who we truly are: infinite and divine souls playing a human game—at least for now. Imagine that you are a magnificent, divine spirit who has lived throughout eternity, and that you know all there is to know. You are part of the Divine Source and you are one with God. You are pure Light and you land on Earth to play the human game of life, trapped in the illusion of limitation because you find yourself in a confined space—a little body. Part of the game is that you are going to forget everything you knew before being human, and you are going to play in this earth plane to experience life and see how fast you can remember the truth of who you were as the magnificent, divine being you started out as. Whew! That was a mouthful. Just imagine what your soul felt like going through it. That is the game we all play here on Earth. We are humans seeking to remember our divinity.

You are in the middle of the maze, and you want to see how fast you can move from the center out into infinity, unity, and divinity. *How fast can I remember who I really am?* Answering that question is why your soul prompts you to seek, question, and yearn to know thyself. You have your own Lords, Masters, Teachers, and Beings of Light that keep your Akashic Record, and they are waiting for you to speak to them so they can help you. They will take your hand and walk you out of the maze and the game of life. All you have to do is ask.

As we connect with the Akashic Records—as we see things from a new perspective and feel it energetically—we move into a higher vibration, which is a healing vibration energy. This Divine Source energy is actually the information arm of God, where the energy of the Akashic Records is stored. When we study our Record, which is one of the highest vibrations, we move into this vibrational field with ease so we can experience profound healing. When we plug into the vibration of the Divine arm, the Akashic Field of energy doesn't only heal us; we also heal the earth plane. As more people study and access the Akashic Records and bring forth that Divine vibration, it will magnify and intensify as higher energy here on Earth as a whole. In other words, as you heal yourself, you will also heal the collective energy of humanity because your healing energy expands out into the ethers. That is how the powerful Akashic Records work as a healing tool.

When I teach or give a presentation on the Akashic Records, I like to begin with the following prayer to help bring the highest vibrational energy to the group. You may want to read it with the same intent to help you gain full understanding from this book:

> *Close your eyes slightly and allow your body to relax into your chair. Just relax into the Akashic Field of energy and allow yourself to feel the sensations going on in your body. It may feel sparkly, tingly, or warm. I often see it as a silvery blue column of light. Whatever it is that you notice is just perfect.*

Now, take a deep breath and allow yourself to drop deeper into your heart by focusing on your heart center. Ask your heart to relax and expand a bit more, similar to a balloon expanding and filling your chest. Feel the warmth. Say:

"We ask our souls, our spirits, to come fully present in our physical bodies. We ask the Divine Lords of unconditional love to help us center fully in this moment as we create this sacred space. Please wrap us in your love and protection and allow us to travel to the highest realm of the Akasha available to us today. Please help us as we lay our multidimensional hearts open to Divine love and release all resistance. Lords of the Akashic Records, please guide us to the deepest truth that we can access now. Support us in healing and releasing that which no longer serves us on our true path. We give great thanks for your Divine love and support on this journey today. And so it is."

As you feel your heart open and see this energy surround you, you may also notice a new lightness or tingly feeling in your body.

Soul Contracts

The Akashic Beings of Light often show me funny images whenever I ask them questions. They are pure Divine love, and often express themselves as joy, fun, and laughter. When I asked them to explain the soul contracts that we write before we are born, they showed me a huge gymnasium—the kind you may have played basketball in when you were in high school. In this gymnasium, many souls came together before their journey back to Earth for another human life. They interacted with each other, much like a networking event. During these interactions, they made arrangements and/or contracts with each other to set up situations in order to complete the karma that their souls intended during any number of lifetimes on earth.

For example, one soul might want to learn forgiveness. Another soul would step up and say, "Hey, I'll agree to be your grouchy, unbearable father, so you'll have lots of chances to learn how to forgive me." And the other soul would say, "Sure, that works. I was pretty awful to you in our last lifetime together, so this will also help complete that karmic circle." Of course, once you land here on Earth, you don't remember any of that, or that these contracts were made in the energy of love and generosity. You may just be wondering, *Why did I end up with such awful parents?*

Even though we may have experienced a lot of trauma in our lives, it has been my experience with those who have worked with the Akashic Records that when they receive a broader understanding of any trauma, the experience can turn out to be quite positive. I often hear reactions such as this: "Wow, okay, so I understand that abusive father was helpful for me to recognize the light that I am, and then to forgive him as a soul, knowing the truth of who he really is. I can feel this information healing a rift in my heart. Thank you, Beings of Light." Another common reaction is, "That feels good to shift the perspective and stop feeling like a victim." My goal with writing *The Infinite Wisdom of the Akashic Records* is to help you achieve that type of realization and the healing that comes with it—seeing the big picture so that you know the truth of who you really are, and to *be* the forgiveness, and the unconditional love that is pure Divine truth. And so that you know throughout your being that this is really what you have come to this Earth to do.

What we find in the Akashic Field is that when we ask a question, such as, "What is this abuse in my life all about?" we will receive two, three, or more layers of information because the Records are so vast with stored information. Let's take an example. The Beings of Light may show you a few lifetimes when you had some unfinished karma with this man that you call your father in this lifetime, and you are shown other past lives in which you acted in the same way as your abusive father. Do you see where you had the opportunity for your turn at being out of balance and abusive to others? They may also show you a lifetime when you were a powerful priestess in a goddess temple at a time when it fell to a warring clan, and you were murdered, so you vowed to never own your power again. Your Record may show that your emotional trauma was triggered yesterday, but it has its roots in an event that occurred 5,000 years ago.

You can use the Records to receive multidimensional, multi-layered answers to work on each piece of the puzzle, and to work on clearing and releasing the karma, vows, and contracts you have with any person, place, or thing. As you go through this book, I will show you how to do this type of work for yourself in your own Akashic Record.

Learning to work in the Akashic Records is a process because it is so expansive in knowledge. Even if the Akashic Beings of Light, Masters, and Teachers give you two layers of one big issue today, you may find that you need to revisit that issue and continue to work with your emotions in a week or a month. We often find that a big issue tends to have multiple layers of emotional pain, with karma attached from at least one lifetime that you came here to complete. These completions can include vows from another lifetime. All of these elements can contribute to the drama and trauma from just one big issue. Sometimes you will have to process and integrate the information you were given before you can go on to the next step or unravel the next layer. When I'm working with clients, we often revisit the same issue by continuing to work through the different layers of that issue. Additional layers can surface with time, but we are not always able to see and clear them all right away. It isn't terribly useful to receive a clairvoyant picture of a traumatic lifetime without an understanding of how to release it through clearing. I always ask the Akashic Beings of Light, "What can I do to clear that?" I'm a channel of healing energy by the nature of my soul lineage, and if you are as well, you'll probably want to look for what you can uplift and clear. This is part of what I'll teach you to do with your Akashic Records throughout this book. It is important to ask, "What can I finish? What is it that I can bring to completion now? What karma or vow is ready to be released?" I found that because my intention is always to heal, complete karma, or release stuck energy, the Beings of Light offer tools to accomplish what is necessary in the healing process. By learning to access your Akashic Record, you will also learn about these tools and how to use them.

An example of a soul contract that is affecting many light workers right now is their contract to help rebalance the masculine/feminine energies on Earth. Each person's soul contract appears differently depending on his or her individual life purpose. I find the Beings of Light of the Akashic Field are telling us repeatedly that it is time to bring much of this karma to completion so that we can be on task for the specific purpose we chose to incarnate. They also say that unless we can really understand and own an issue or emotion before we clear it, we will continue to re-create and repeat some of those patterns. There are times when we can clear an old energy, but it isn't beneficial because we don't understand it. We haven't moved to the next level to embody the realizations. One of our souls' reasons for coming to Earth is to grow and learn from our experiences. We come to experience the beauty and wonder of the Earth and to remember the truth of who we are. We are ancient, wise, and eternal beings, and we desire to bring that truth to humanity through ourselves. It's as though we are climbing a long and winding staircase to enlightenment, which is the remembering of the truth of our infinite selves. If we skip a lot of stairs on our journey, we may tumble back down again to where we were, or even a bit below. The Beings of Light say that when we "magically" heal without the learning, we don't acquire the growth and wisdom and we're stuck on a step mid-staircase.

When working in the Akashic Records, we work with a deep sense of integrity toward the information we receive. While doing our work with the Beings of Light, Masters, and Teachers it becomes important for us to understand our motivation behind the questions we are asking, in order to fully integrate the answers we receive. We are learning on many levels, and the answers are not as simple as *yes* and *no*. Working in the Akashic Records quickens our understanding of ourselves and the patterns of behavior we use in our everyday life. The teachings received from the Records facilitate personal and spiritual growth, so that we can move into a place of unconditional love and forgiveness for ourselves and for humanity.

The formation of this book, *The Infinite Wisdom of the Akashic Records*, is a perfect example of how working in the Akashic Records with a desire to serve creates the purpose, focus, and essence of healing yourself and others. You never know where your work in the Records will lead you. My Akashic Record school, the Akashic Knowing School of Wisdom, is another manifestation I realized with the help of the Beings of Light.

I know personally that when we can learn to forgive ourselves of real, forgotten, or imagined transgressions, moving on in our lives into a bigger picture of our work in the world is much easier because we are filled with and live in a space of unconditional love. As we do that, we are offering support to humanity and helping the Earth to awaken into a state of unity and enlightenment. Isn't it astonishing to know that you can help to raise humanity's and the Earth's vibration into a more loving presence, just by learning about yourself through opening your own Akashic Record, while sitting in your living room? How miraculous is that? The Beings of Light tell us that working diligently in the Akashic Field offers its own path to enlightenment. By living in the very high vibration—by learning, growing, and expanding multidimensionally in this amazing energy—you are awakening by creating a deeply connected place in which to view and live in the world. As you do this, you are being awakened to the essence of your being and purpose on this earth plane, so that you can fully participate in creating a new world of love and peace—a heaven on earth.

Money Nightmares

As I've worked with thousands of clients throughout the years, I've heard about many kinds of money nightmares. I've helped people who work so hard at creating their business only to end in a legal battle with a partner and eventual bankruptcy. I've helped others who fear leaving the corporate world to follow their hearts on their soul path. This often causes trauma in their everyday life, sometimes leading to divorce and physical illness. Sometimes we do follow our hearts, but end up struggling with everything breaking down until we lose every bit of money we make to repairs on our cars, houses, and bodies.

Money has many layers from a spiritual perspective, because we are complex human beings and we complicate money's meaning and significance in our lives. One of the greatest gifts we receive when we learn to open our own Akashic Record is the realization of how expansive we are as souls, how many lifetimes we have lived, and all of the challenges we've overcome and grown from throughout all of those lifetimes, all the way through to who you are today, right now, reading this book. We begin to realize in a very palpable way that we are infinite beings living for a short time in our physical bodies, which is so small compared to our expansive soul. When we work on our money issues with the help of the Akashic Records, we aren't simply working through one of our money stories—we could have five, 10, 50, or thousands of stories involving a monetary theme. Monetary themes come from our families, our teachers, and our cultural, social, or religious beliefs. Just imagine all of the unspoken beliefs about money we've picked up along the way as we were growing up.

Add to this lifetime, ancestral monetary beliefs from your numerous lifetimes when you were financially challenged. We all have different and fascinating stories about money, all written in our Akashic Records. Wouldn't it be valuable to learn about the lifetimes in which you were rich, generous, and powerful, so that you can tap into that wisdom?

These multiple pieces of the puzzle called our "life" come into our energy field from past and present lifetimes, and create complex layers with energetic blocks. The way the Akashic Beings of Light have explained our ancestral energy is that, whatever our ancestors experienced, felt, and did is passed on through our DNA, affecting us in this lifetime. Of course, we are not experiencing all of the ancestral challenges, only the ones that help us accomplish our soul's contract in our present life. We absorb many of our parents' and grandparents' money energies (good or bad), as well as those of other people, such as teachers, who had an influence on our learning and patterned our ways of thinking. Often, what they said through words or body language, or how they felt about money and its purpose—for example, "rich people are selfish," or, "money is the root of all evil"—may still influence us today. We all connect energetically into the collective unconscious, and we often unknowingly believe that those thoughts and attitudes are our true beliefs and values, when in fact they are not.

As you work in your Akashic Record as taught here, you will be able to ask the Beings of Light to assist with specific tools that will be useful as you move through your questions. I will be guiding you through the process step by step, just as I do with the students of my Akashic Knowing School of Wisdom. You will learn how to formulate questions so that you can receive the most information with the greatest clarity and understanding. One of my favorite questions that helps my students find the necessary tools for their healing work quickly is, "How do I clear my family's attitudes and ancestral energy from my energy field and life?"

When we open our personal Akashic Record and start to look at our past lives, we may learn that in certain lifetimes we had taken strict vows of poverty. For example, you could have been an ascetic in India, a nun in Spain, or a monk in Tibet. If you are having financial fears or difficulty with attracting money, you may be unknowingly hanging on to a variety of vows of poverty. You will want to work on those right away, once you have gotten the hang of opening your own Akashic Record. The Beings of Light can take you back into the energy of that past life so they can clear and release any of those old vows, allowing you to reclaim the positive spiritual energy and wisdom that was trapped from that lifetime. It's possible to move in and out of multidimensional time and space in the Akashic Field. There, we can heal a past life to create an energy shift in our present time. When we heal that past life, there will literally be an energetic shift right now—in our life, in this moment. Often times, you will feel it immediately. Sometimes it takes us a bit of time to allow the energy to be integrated in our consciousness. Either way, the energy will shift. All you have to do is let it happen and notice the transformations.

Another common scenario that comes up when working with money nightmares in the Akashic Records is a past life in which you were wealthy but were not a kind or generous person. A past-life image will show up of a king sitting in a room of gold, all alone, because everyone hates him and he has lost all of his friends and family. He has taxed his subjects into extreme poverty and can't even pay for someone to care for him. The king dies alone, with nothing or nobody other than his money and his guilt to keep him company. On his deathbed, suffering alone, he vows never to be wealthy again. He decides money has made him a bad person and blames his painful death and loneliness not on himself, but on money! If you want to release the old money energy so that you can start receiving your abundance, it's important to heal and clear traumas from past-life vows. Deathbed vows, in particular, will often stick with us for many, many, many lives.

Health Worries

As with most issues, health challenges are usually multilayered. The pain you are feeling may not even be your own, because other people's energy also affects you, positively or negatively. We unconsciously take on and carry around other people's energy; that is why it is important to create healthy boundaries. The tools I'll teach you are designed to help you learn how to clear the layers of negative energy that you may be experiencing, including moving other people's energy out of your space.

I know from personal experience that health issues can arise when we are not listening to or following our soul's path. When I was 20 years old, I decided I wasn't going to follow the soul's path that I had been aware of since I was 3 years old. I chose instead to take the good-time-party road in San Francisco in the 1970s and '80s. I walked away from what was a very clear soul path, filled with spiritual awareness and understanding, because I was in deep emotional pain. Instead of working through the pain, understanding it, and growing from it, I ran away to what appeared to be an easy escape—good times in San Francisco. It took about 15 years of ignoring my body's physical symptoms for me to realize that I had created severe chronic fatigue, and that I had to immediately change my lifestyle. I made a conscious decision to end the wild partying and move back onto my soul path to heal myself.

Of course, there are many reasons to have physical pain; most are in this physical realm but many have layers in other times and dimensions. Sometimes, energy bleeds through from a past-life wound to our current life, and it can manifest physically. For instance, a person will literally feel a pain in his or her back or shoulder in the area where he or she had been stabbed in a past life. The energy of the pain can be cleared from the past life through the Akashic Records, giving the person immediate pain relief. I will show you techniques to help you work with these different layers of energy. What I find so fascinating about working in the Records is that these layers of energy are often connected to the reason why we came here at this time. So, whether it is money energy you wrestle with or health issues, the past-life energy that you contracted to release in this life will continue to cause you problems until you can somehow come to a place of remembrance, releasing, and then recycling the old energy.

Weight Concerns

Many people's lifetimes have been filled with struggle, poverty, and starvation. A past-life vow never to starve again can play a significant role in a weight struggle in this life. If you gain weight no matter what you eat or don't eat, a past-life vow could be lurking behind the weight. I definitely don't advocate ignoring scientific reasons behind health issues and weight gain or loss, but I have often found added layers in the Akashic realm that it helps to clear.

You could find that your weight is connected to three or more layers such as these:

- **Layer One:** A past-life vow to never starve again.

- **Layer Two:** An energy program that originated from childhood. The little girl who is still trying to fulfill her mother's ideal image of the perfect daughter. This internal push and pull has led to overeating and a struggle with bulimia as an adult, but the energy is stuck in the inner child realm.

- **Layer Three:** Self-esteem and the challenge to feel good about yourself no matter the outward appearance. This may originate in a past life and be connected to this current life's theme related to food and self-esteem, making this even more multi-layered.

The Akashic Records are such a vast body of information and wisdom. The more time you spend in learning how to ask the right questions, the easier it will be to access the information you seek, with greater understanding and clarity. I also suggest that you make a habit of accessing your Akashic Record daily. Practice. Practice. Practice. The more you practice, the easier it will be for you to work through the various layers of energy ready to be released.

Forgiveness

One of the greatest challenges we, as humans, face in our lives is the ability to forgive. There are so many reasons in our human existence for us to hold on to anger, resentment, and passive-aggressive be-haviors. It is in our greatest challenges where we find ourselves at major crossroads. If we are conscious in our choices, we will ask ourselves, *Do I take the road of forgiveness and release myself from the bondage of anger, or do I stay in the cycle of anger and remain destined to repeat this challenge once again?* I asked the Beings of Light for a special prayer to help my students access forgiveness easily and effortlessly, and so I was given the Forgiveness Prayer, which is a valuable tool to clear the layers that might be affecting your relation-ships with people, money, health, and weight. This invocation was given through the Akashic Records to help clear any karma from lessons you have already learned or need to complete. The Beings of Light gave us this prayer to help ease the pain that humans tend to endure rather than release in their lives. It's time for you to release any old energy you have been holding on to from any issues you may be stuck in. A helpful hint for you to find out if you are stuck in a lack-of-forgiveness pattern is to notice when you are repeating familiar and comfortable ways of dealing with stressful situations. You will want to pay close attention to how you feel and what you are thinking when these patterns come up for you. Then use the Forgiveness Prayer to assist you in releasing those old patterns.

Keep this prayer with you at all times. You can share it with anyone you feel may need it. As you read this prayer, please be sure to center yourself fully in your heart energy.

THE FORGIVENESS PRAYER

Divine, Spirit, Source, please move me into a state of forgiveness toward anyone or anything that has hurt me, consciously or unconsciously, from the beginning of time to this present moment. I now forgive them and I release the energy of the past.

Divine, Spirit, Source, please move me into a state of forgiveness toward myself for any hurt that I have caused others, consciously or unconsciously, from the beginning of time to this present moment. I now forgive myself and I release the energy of the past.

Divine, Spirit, Source, please move me into a state of forgiveness toward myself for any hurt that I have caused myself, consciously or unconsciously, from the beginning of time to this present moment. I now forgive myself and release the energy of the past.

I invoke the grace and power of forgiveness to transform my body, mind, and heart as I return to a state of Divine innocence. And so it is.

Chapter 2

Support for Your Life

A Personal Story

Now that you know a little bit about the Akashic Records, I'll share with you the way I actually got into this work, and then we'll start teaching you how to open your own Akashic Record.

I was born into this body "awake." I know you are probably wondering, *What does that mean?* Well, when I was about 3 years old, I had the shocking realization that my spirit had embodied *again*! I remember looking at my hands and thinking, *Oh my gosh, what am I doing here again?* I was also flooded with memories of the energies, feelings, and even some images of when I was not living in a physical human body, but was instead "being" with spirits on another plane. I remembered that when I was on that other plane, I didn't have to work so darn hard at talking and communicating with other beings. Just think about children who are 1, 2, and 3 years old—for them to learn to speak a language and to communicate effectively is a long process and a lot of work. That was my first remembered experience. It's not so uncommon for children at a young age to start having memories of when they could communicate energetically or telepathically. The struggle to learn a language appears to trigger the life-between-life memory in them.

My parents thought I was a little eccentric. I used to tell them I wanted to go home. My mother thought that my request was highly unusual because I was already home, at least in her opinion. Both of my parents were agnostics, so neither one of them was a believer in organized religion. My mother believed that when you died, that was it. You were dead, and you weren't coming back to human form. Ashes to ashes; that was that. My father had an interest in the esoteric spiritual world, which turned out to serve me well on my own spiritual path. For me, it worked out to be a perfect family to be born into because I didn't have much religious training, which meant that I didn't have to do a lot of healing related to religious dogma.

Luckily, when I moved to California in my teens, books related to spiritual growth and Eastern religion were plentiful there. *Be Here Now*, by Baba Ram Dass, was newly available. I also read Robert Monroe's *Journeys Out of the Body*; he was talking about astral-projecting and parallel universes. And then there was Carlos Castaneda, who wrote about his experience of studying with a Shaman in Mexico. All of these books and authors made for expansive and interesting reading for a teenager. I went on to minor in philosophy in college, and I read a lot of books about different religions, including Eastern religions and philosophies. The next part of my education started when I was a bit older, when I met a wonderful psychic teacher with whom I studied for about six years. She was fabulous because she really taught a lot about psychic anatomy and a wide scope of healing energies. I learned so much from her, even though I discovered I wasn't a great psychic. It just didn't work with my intuitive knowing. But something would occasionally happen when I did a psychic reading: I would hear a big, booming voice. It was fascinating, and I'd always think, *Wow, this is the most powerful information*, or, *This is the biggest view of this issue I've ever seen*. I would be shown a very large vision of my client's life. The information would be multilayered. I'd receive answers to the client's questions plus information about how it was connected to a soul contract or karma he or she had come to complete. I also received baby steps to share with clients about how to move forward or shift their perception of the situation. That voice showed up in many of my energy healing and intuitive readings for about five years, but I never knew where it came from. It brought forth fascinating information for me to deliver to my clients, and I never thought to ask with whom I was speaking. What I did notice was that the energy during the reading was different whenever I would receive this vaster, more powerful, and deeper information, but connecting to the booming voice was a frustrating hit-or-miss experience for me. I didn't know of an easy entrance to this realm. I didn't even know what the realm *was*.

My years of psychic training had taught me that after I'd finished clearing old energy for my clients, I was to always ask for the highest and best information that my client could receive from his or her Akashic Record. So of course I was aware that I was accessing the Akashic Records, but it was always from a distance, and with the belief that I was not allowed to enter that realm. Unbeknownst to me, the Beings of Light and the Lords of the Akashic Records were speaking to me and trying to get my attention, but because I never asked, *To whom does this booming voice belong?* I didn't connect it to the Akashic Field.

Then one day when I was at a retreat in Sedona, Arizona, I met a woman who was giving a lecture on medical intuition. I was interested in her talk because of all of the deep work I had done related to my chronic fatigue illness. She also mentioned the Akashic Records, but I thought, *I know all about them.* My psychic teacher had taught me that I could go up to the gate of the Akashic Records to ask the Beings of Light for the information and energy for my clients after I had done a healing on them, but I wasn't allowed inside. I imagined the Akashic Records as a big stone library with giant stone slab steps and a beautiful iron gate around it. The other students and I were taught it was not our business to know what the information or energy was about that was coming to the client from his or her Akashic Record. The interesting thing was, I would clairvoyantly see the energy come down into my client. I would see this energy come down from above, and go into the client's crown chakra and down into his body; sometimes it would fill up his body, and sometimes it would go to a specific area. I had nothing to do with the energy or where it went. I was not controlling it. My responsibility was to ask that it go to the highest and best place where that energy or information would best serve my client.

When I met this woman on my retreat in Sedona, she told me that she was an Akashic Records consultant and that she could access my Akashic Record to give me a reading. I was surprised because, up until that moment, I didn't know that was possible. I was excited at the prospect, and immediately said yes. She gave me an amazing Akashic Record consultation that lasted a couple of hours. The Lords of the Akashic Records came through her in a clear and loud voice to say, *Finally, we've consciously gotten your ear. It's on your soul path to bring this information out into the world, and to use this wisdom for humanity.* By going to that retreat and meeting her, my life changed in a couple of hours. I had gotten my breakthrough on who that loud voice belonged to, and I also received my opportunity to finally enter into the Akashic Records.

Because the consultant I met wasn't a teacher, she connected me to the group of Akashic Records teachers who had taught her the Sacred Prayer she had used to open my Akashic Record. I immediately signed up for a class with their organization. I soon advanced to becoming a consultant, and then I became a teacher. I was also Vice President of their Board of Directors for a few years. They are an amazing group of people and I will forever be grateful to those teachers for sharing this amazing gift with me. And I haven't stopped following guidance of the Lords, Masters, and Teachers of the Akashic Records since.

A day came when the Beings of Light told me it was time to open my own Akashic school, and that they would give me prayers specifically to be taught through my school. They told me that my soul lineage is galactic, and that I had lived on and traveled through many planets and dimensions. I was elated to be given this responsibility. The Akashic Lords told me, *These new prayers will connect to a different lineage of souls that are looking for Akashic access.* They proceeded to give me six new sacred prayers that were related to different soul lineages. A soul lineage traces the path your soul has taken throughout time, and it supports your soul's purpose in this lifetime. For instance, if you lived on scientific planets for many of your lifetimes, your soul purpose now, in this lifetime, may be to bring new technology to Earth or develop new scientific information that may change the way we study an illness, such as cancer. The six prayers are each unique, as they resonate with different people at their soul level, and assist them in remembering some of their unique soul wisdom.

Noticing which prayer or prayers works for you is fun, fascinating, and informative. You will begin by working with three of the prayers in a methodical way. You will ask questions about each of the prayers, as you open them to feel their distinct energies. Then you can pick the one that resonates the most with you. Don't be concerned that you won't be able to tell the difference, because you will. They each resonate at a different frequency, just as each individual person does. So have fun. It is also common to find that different prayers work for you at different times in your life and in different situations you may encounter. Many students have noticed that they may use one prayer for daily types of questions, such as, "How can I organize my day?" Or, "Is there a way for me to be of service to my community today?" They may decide to pick another prayer for a question about their past lives. I will tell you more about that as you work through the different processes in this book, and as you learn how to access your own Akashic Record more and more deeply.

The fascinating thing about the Akashic Records is that they are infinite. If you were drawn to read this book and take part in its exercises, please know that you are a very ancient being and that your Record is vast. In this book you will work with three of the prayers that connect to different planets, dimensions, and lineages. You will learn to trust the information you're receiving through your Akashic Record through practice and patience.

Getting Prepared

The process of learning *anything* is typically quite individual, so you will learn at your own pace, and in your own special way. If you're finding that you are having difficulty opening your Record, or aren't sure when and if you are in your Record, don't give up! Even if you aren't feeling clear about what's happening, just be patient with yourself and the process because your efforts to access the Akashic Records are significant. You are opening an important door to information, and you will see progress as you proceed through this book, as I teach you how to ask questions that will take you exactly where you want to go in your personal Record.

Throughout the book, I will be talking about the Akashic Records themselves, as well as the healing prayers and tools that were given to me by the Akashic Beings of Light in order to help you on your journey with ease and love. These tools and prayers are designed to assist you in healing yourself, your life, your karma, and your soul contracts. The Beings of Light want to provide you with support for your life, and they want you to access the wisdom that will help you. I'm here to help them help you, so allow yourself to relax into the energy of the Akashic Field, and to feel and accept their support and unconditional love as you read this book.

I teach a four-course series on the Akashic Records, and what you're learning here is an introduction to the Records similar to my Course 1. In that course, I teach students to access their personal Akashic Record and how to use it to support and transform their daily life. They also learn many tools to come present into their body so they can create and manifest the life their soul intends.

In Course 2, my students deepen their ability to access their personal Akashic Record. As I've mentioned, one's Akashic Record is expansive, and in Course 2, we work more with our ancestral lineage, soul lineage, genetic lineage, creativity, and, of course, our past lives, because there is so much in our past lives that affects us in this lifetime. It is very important for us to know what we came to learn about in this lifetime, so we can work through it, reclaim it, and utilize it.

In Course 3, students learn to access the Akashic Record of others, which means that they can actually start to do Akashic Record consultations. Sometimes people who take this course are looking for a new career, to deepen into the Akashic world and to use it for humanity. I have many students who are learning to access the Records for others, but many take the third course even if they're not particularly interested in doing consultations because it also greatly strengthens their trust in the information they receive in the Records. What you find is that everyone's Akashic Records are a little different. Your Lords, your Beings of Light, your Teachers, they're *yours*, and so the flavor of each person's Akashic Record is distinct.

You are a unique individual, and each individual's Akashic Record mirrors his or her uniqueness. When you start to access the Records for other people, you begin to notice these differences, as well as the similarities of being in your Record and theirs. For example, when consulting the Akashic Records for different people, you may be much more clairvoyant and see a lot of images and pictures for one person rather than another, or even than your own Record. You may experience clairsentience in someone's Akashic Record who is energetically a more sensitive person. That means that he or she *feels* the information more than hears it clairaudiently, or sees it clairvoyantly. As a result, learning to access the Akashic Records of others offers you numerous opportunities to gain a lot of experience, information, and depth. You will learn from your own experiences just how rewarding it is to work with the Masters and Teachers; that, I can just about guarantee. Once you do, you will want to share this work with everyone.

Course 4 is Certified Consultant Training, so if you're really interested in doing this professionally, it's wonderful to be a Certified Akashic Records Consultant. The course is also filled with advanced healing tools that you can use for yourself and for your clients. These tools come from my 20 years of work as an energy healer, working with a large variety of modalities. It's about a six-month process from Course 3, Learning to Access the Akashic Record for Others, to becoming a Certified Consultant. If you're interested, please go to *www.akashicknowing.com* to read about the different courses and how you can sign up for a class remotely or in person. I mentioned the different courses so that you have a better understanding of where you are in the learning process, and what your next step in the process can be, if you desire to work at a deeper level in the Records.

Guided, Guarded, and Protected

When I teach my Akashic Records classes, we do a guided meditation called "Guided, Guarded, and Protected." I also refer to it as the "Golden Egg" meditation. You can download this meditation—my gift to you—on my Website at *TheInfiniteWisdom.com/goldenegg*. It's a wonderful way to become centered in your body and to fill yourself up with your highest and best vibration. It actually protects you because you become solid from the inside out, which is a wonderful way to start creating boundaries for and around yourself.

The Importance of Being Grounded

At minimum, please take a moment to center and ground yourself before you open your Akashic Record. Doing so makes it much easier to be clear when you open your Record because you've moved everyone out of your space, and you become centered in your heart. Grounding is a profound process for many reasons. Most people are unaware of it, but we often resist being in the body because it can feel heavy, dense, and emotional. Those are not pleasant sensations for many people. It's much denser than we're used to as light beings, but if you can truly learn to ground, it can change your life.

Here are some benefits of being grounded:

✦ It puts you in present time, so you're not living in the past or future.

✦ It helps you to manifest your dreams. Unless you're in present time and in your body, it's very hard to create in the present moment. All our intentions are just that—intentions—unless we have the physical energy to create them now.

✦ When you and your client are both grounded, it helps the client to hear your message in a consultation.

Kite Meditation

Most people only come down into their heart chakra and no further, but it's in our 3rd chakra, the solar plexus, that we do much of our creating on this earth plane. This is a meditation you can practice yourself and do with clients to get them grounded.

+ Start with your eyes closed.
+ Imagine a kite in the shape of a body with a long tail flying over your head.
+ Grab hold of the kite tail, and gently pull it down into your body.
+ Imagine it coming in all the way to your toes, filling your body.
+ The tail becomes a grounding cord coming from the base of your spine, just like a monkey's tail would.
+ This tails grows long, deep to the center of the Earth.
+ See your tail wrapping around the core of the Earth in a solidly grounded hold.
+ Feel yourself full of your own energy.
+ Sit with this feeling for a few minutes.

Your Heart's Desire

Consider why your heart has called you to this work in the Akashic Field. Spend a few moments thinking about it, and then write down three to five reasons why your heart has called you to access your Record. By combining the high-vibrational Akashic Field energy with the vibration of your heart's desires, the Akashic Field energy is literally becoming grounded here in physical form, which makes it so much easier to manifest your desires.

Now that you've considered your heart's desire, take a moment to write down three to five things that you wish to receive from your Akashic Record. Do you want to clear out past karma? Resolve an issue with a family member? Deal with a health concern? In what areas do you wish to receive guidance? Your Akashic Record is a vast, infinite field, so it becomes critical to learn to ask useful and efficient questions. There is an art to formulating your questions, so practice, practice, practice. In your work in the Records, you will receive information that can help you to take steps forward and to make choices that are in your highest and best interests. Yes-or-no questions offer only simple answers, so always reframe your questions to allow for answers with more depth of information.

Here's an example of the importance of asking the right questions. I had a client who came to me for an Akashic Records consultation. She had been divorced for about three years and was ready for a new relationship, and so her questions revolved around that: "Will I have a new boyfriend? When will a new relationship start?" I'd been working with her for about a year, and she continued to ask these types of questions along with deeper, life-changing ones. One time she asked, "When, when, when? When will

I meet a guy?" I immediately saw an image. It looked like a man in a Polaroid picture. It was startling to me because it was so specific, right down to the man's hairstyle, including a little bald patch, his red-and-black plaid shirt, and his black pickup truck. I said, "Wow, this is astonishing, just like a real photo of somebody. I rarely see like that." We were both excited about this information.

She kept asking when she would meet her man. The answer I received for her was "within the next two months, and this is kind of what he's going to look like." About three weeks later, she called me and said, "I met him and he looks just like the picture you saw. He even drives a pickup truck. We just fell madly, crazy in love. It's just wonderful and I'm so excited! Everything is great. Thank you, thank you!" Of course I thought, *Wow! This is terrific and quite useful.* A few weeks went by, and she called again to say that something had gone wrong. "I feel like I'm his mother," she said. "He is super needy. How did this happen? Why didn't they tell me? What's wrong with this picture? This isn't a soul mate." And I said, "Oh, interesting, let's think back." I said, "Did you ask, 'When will I meet my soul partner, the highest and best partner for me? When will I meet the gentleman who is on a spiritual path similar to mine? When will I meet this man who will hold me in love and integrity and support me on my path?'? Did we ask any of those questions?" Hmm...no, the question was, "When will I meet a guy?" It's the client's responsibility to ask the question, though we as consultants do our best to help and guide them. For me, it was a great learning experience. It's easy in our very human state to say, "I'm ready for a relationship. When is it going to show up?" But if you truly want a partner to walk your spiritual path and support you in your life, then you must ask deeper questions. One of the things you want to start to think about as you work in your Akashic Record is how you will ask a question. Also think about what your intention is, and what kind of energy is behind your questions.

Take a few minutes to write out some questions about your wishes and desires, such as, "How can I fulfill my desire?" Or, "What is holding me back from having, creating, or receiving my heart's desire? Is there a higher or better intention for me?" Remember that you're not in your Akashic Record yet. Asking those questions first outside of your Record, and *then* inside your Record, is the perfect way to start to see the difference in information you receive when you work within your Akashic Record. With this process you will start to dig deep into its energy to experience a greater depth of information.

Guidelines for Accessing Your Record

Following are some guidelines to keep you protected and guided. They are not meant to be a rigid doctrine, but rather to help you grow and learn through the Records without getting in your own way.

✦ **Be present and consciously in your body. Keep your eyes open as much as possible. You want to learn to walk through life—and also in your Akashic Record—with your eyes wide open.** I know this is a challenge for those of you who are clairvoyant. Clairvoyants often tell me that it's hard to "see" when their eyes are open. For that, I suggest a couple of things. You can go ahead and shut your eyes for a minute or two, see a picture, obtain some information, and then open your eyes again. I also like to suggest you use a blank wall, so that you can gaze at the wall with your soft, open eyes, and learn to see images and pictures in your mind's eye. I've personally learned to "see" clairvoyantly with my eyes open. I don't mean that I am seeing the images in the physical realm; I am seeing in my mind's eye with my eyes open. Because you'll be working with journaling as a process to access your Record, you'll notice it's pretty darn hard to write with your eyes closed.

The Beings of Light have told us that to create heaven on earth, it's important to be guided in our daily lives. That means opening your Record often during the day. Create a daily habit of it because this process works beautifully when you integrate it into your life and work. That's one of the reasons I highly recommend practicing opening your Record to receive information, and hearing, feeling, seeing, knowing, and using all of your different intuitive skills and senses with your eyes open.

✦ **Use your first, middle, and last legal name to open your Akashic Record.** Use the name that is on your driver's license or your passport. Don't necessarily use your maiden name or birth name. It's the present-day, legal name that works best. I've had students who go by spiritual names for many years, and students who have used family nicknames all of their lives, but when they start to access their Record, they realize those non-legal names don't hold their complete Record. They find that their legal name accesses their vast Akashic Record, and their nickname or spiritual name only accesses a portion of it.

✦ **Always read the prayers; you do not need to memorize them.** The words are symbols, which hold a vibration. Seeing, reading, and hearing the words will add levels of energy to the prayers. We literally read a prayer out loud so we can see it, hear it, and feel its energy all at once. The vibration of the words is received in our ears, just like a tone, while the letters and words are energetic symbols. Those are all important and powerful components of this vibrational key, because opening the Record isn't just a wishful dream, it's actually possible. We need to have that key cut just right, and to use it in a particular fashion to access the Records.

✦ **Be deliberate in your quest for answers; it will deepen your reception of the information.** The process you will learn is based on asking questions that will take you to the area of your Record that you wish to explore. It's useful to write five to seven questions on one issue that you wish to delve into deeply. This process of asking questions is like a maypole dance. A maypole dance uses a tall pole in the middle of a field. Hanging from the top of the maypole are a variety of colored ribbons. During the May celebration, dancers each hold a ribbon while dancing specific steps so that they go in and out and around each other, weaving the ribbons around the maypole. This creates a beautiful fabric with all of the multicolored ribbons—the full expression of the ribbons. That's what you are doing with multiple questions on one topic.

Imagine the maypole as the issue that you want to work on, and that the questions you ask are your colored ribbons. As you ask each question, you're receiving different pieces of your puzzle. You're touching on numerous facets of that one issue. By asking numerous questions, you're perceiving a complete answer, instead of a myopic answer. Consider the example I gave you about the woman looking for a relationship. What if she had asked if there is a soul partner for her? Or if she had asked, "Is there someone with a high spiritual soul contract with me? Is there someone who has a contract to support me?" All of those types of questions would have been more useful to her than, "Is there a guy? Yes or no." It's important to stay away from yes-or-no questions. The answer can be misleading, as we saw in that case.

✦ **Accountability to your own integrity while working in the Akashic Record is vital.** Ask questions for and about yourself, not others. Trust me when I say, as you are working in your Record, learning about the different aspects of yourself, there will be plenty of questions to ask about yourself! This is an important point as you start to work in your personal Record. Learning to access the Akashic Records is a time for *you*. Now you are able to focus on who you are, and learn about areas of your life that have been stopping you from achieving your goals or finding your heartfelt life purpose. This work right now is all about you: Why did you choose this life? Why did you choose this family? What's your next best step? Is there something you could know or clear? What is causing your fear or holding you back? Do you have a soul contract that would be useful to work with?

At this phase, you never ask questions about other people. As curious as you may be, it is invasive, and their information is not in your Record. Questions such as, "Is my teenager smoking pot?" or, "Is my husband having an affair?" or, "Is my friend talking behind my back?" are questions outside of your integrity when working in the Akashic Records. You can ask, "How can I be the best parent to my teenager?" or, "What blocks me from feeling close to my husband?" This process is based on you asking the questions that will take *you* into areas of *your* Record that you wish to explore, so that you can expand your spiritual growth on your soul path.

✦ **Please carry the sacred Akashic prayers with you so that you can access your Records whenever you desire.** Some students take a photo with their phone so they always have access to their Records. Most of my students who delve deeply into this work really want to access the Records all the time, so it's beneficial to keep the prayers with you.

✦ **Please do not teach these Akashic Record prayers to anyone without proper teacher training.** It takes time to become a teacher and to become proficient in this work. When I train my teachers, they understand the high level of responsibility they are accepting when they teach others to access the Akashic Field. These prayers seem simple to learn, but do not let that fool you; they are extremely powerful. Consultants advancing to teachers understand the karma they could inflict if they are careless and disrespectful of these Akashic Record prayers. It really doesn't honor the Akashic Record, or the healing prayers, if you quickly explain them to a friend. Sometimes we are so excited about our new wisdom that we want to share it with everyone. I would ask that if there is anyone interested in doing this work, that you send them to my Website to find a live class, or gift them with a copy of *The Infinite Wisdom of the Akashic Records.*

✦ **I recommend you open your Akashic Record daily for the next month, and write down your insights by journaling.** Begin with 15 minutes and increase your writing time whenever possible. Accessing your Record and learning to go deeper is similar to becoming used to physical exercise—you need to build up over time. For many, in the beginning it's physically tiring to be in the Records for a long time because we aren't used to the high vibration.

At the very least, please open your Record a couple of times a week, because that's the only way you will become proficient at this work. It's a phenomenally powerful tool, but it does take practice.

I know your schedule is packed, so remember that accessing your Record is, in fact, a useful and often timesaving tool. For example, you can ask a question or two about how to organize your day ("Should I take a different route to work?" "Should I change up my morning routine?") or whether doing something new and different is in your highest and best interests ("What's the best outfit to wear to acquire the job I want?").

✦ **Alcohol and drugs lower your vibration, so I suggest refraining from opening your Record until any substance has had time to clear out of your body completely, usually eight to 12 hours.** Prescription medications are acceptable, although painkillers and sleeping aids will also lower your vibration. So please just be aware of this, because it can affect the quality of information you will receive. A lower vibration makes it much harder to access the Records because you're starting from a lower energetic place, trying to make that leap into a very high vibration. Think of it as trying to skip up four steps at a time. It's a pretty unlikely leap for most of us, so start in a healthy and clear state to make accessing your Record easier.

+ **Please do not drive a car with your Record open.** Working with your Record can really space you out, especially in the beginning. Most of the time, the Beings of Light will not even speak to us while we're driving because we're unable to listen and take notes. The information might be lost and forgotten if we have our Record open while driving. Even though you are consciously aware inside the Record, you are in a somewhat altered state. You may even notice that you start to feel tired, most especially when you close the Record. On the other hand, some of my students find that when they start accessing the Akashic Records, their energy level rises. Just remember: Records and driving do not mix, so please, be safe and do not do it.

+ **Give your body time.** Being in the Records is like exercising; when I don't exercise for a long time, and then I do yoga, I tend to feel more tired instead of rejuvenated. It may take me a few weeks, or even a month, until I build up my stamina again to receive that energy boost from exercise. Working with your Akashic Record is similar to exercising in that way. We're learning to access a higher vibration and to hold it in our physical bodies. Our bodies do not normally vibrate at such a high frequency, so it takes time to grow used to that new high vibration. Our bodies are actually clearing lower vibrations, which can contribute to the tiredness. Think of a light bulb: outside your Record you are a 30-watt bulb; inside your Record you are a 200-watt bulb. And when you close your Record, it takes time for your wattage to lower.

Three Akashic Prayers
Outside of the Records

You will start by working with three different prayers *outside* of your Record, because I want you to feel the energy intuitively first, by using your clairsentience. Then you will use my **Akashic Knowing Wisdom Prayer System**, a step-by-step process, to go *inside* your Record. The following exercise will help you understand the difference between the two processes.

In the exercise, you will find four simple questions after each prayer that will help you to sense intuitively your connection to each prayer. Because *you will not have your Record open*, pay close attention to the quality and depth of the information you are intuitively receiving. You will be able to make a comparison once you actually go inside your Record, but for now, just do it intuitively. Take the time to write down what you are feeling energetically, and any information that you are receiving. Also, write about your experiences. It's quite validating to be able to read your journal entries about what you received intuitively *outside* the Record. This process will help you as you move on to the **Akashic Knowing Wisdom Prayer System** for opening the Records.

Your instructions for using the three prayers *outside* of the Akashic Record are as follows:

1. Read the prayer.

2. Ask yourself questions 1 through 4.

3. Write in your journal what you feel, receive, and experience.

4. Move on to the next prayer.

PRAYER 1

Divine Beings of Light of Unconditional Love, help me to center fully in this moment as I create this sacred space. Please wrap me in your Love, and allow me to travel to the highest realms of the Akasha available to me today.

Lords, Masters, and Teachers, I ask that you show me what it feels like to be a clear channel of my Akashic Record.

> *Beings of Light, please guide me to the deepest Truth of me. Support me in healing and releasing the appropriate karma and contracts that have brought me to this life. I give great thanks for your Divine love, support, and protection on this journey.*

Now answer the following questions:

1. How does my body feel when I read this prayer?

2. Is there an emotional connection to this prayer? Do I feel it in my heart or gut?

3. What am I thinking? Where does my mind go?

4. Do I receive any images or pictures with this prayer?

PRAYER 2

> *Akashic Lords, please help me to lay my multidimensional heart open to Divine love, as I lay down all resistance. I ask the Lords, Masters, and Teachers of me to align me with you, in my Akashic Record.*

> *Beings of Light of my Akashic Record, please show me the way to deepen into the Truth of my soul.*

> *Please keep me safe and protected as I access Divine soul wisdom and information in my Akashic realm.*

Now answer the following questions:

1. How does my body feel when I read this prayer?
2. Is there an emotional connection to this prayer? Do I feel it in my heart or gut?
3. What am I thinking? Where does my mind go?
4. Do I receive any images or pictures with this prayer?

PRAYER 3

Divine Mother, Father, All that Is, please expand my state of consciousness and move me into Divine alignment with my Akashic Record.

I ask that the shields of protection be activated to encircle me as I move deeply into my Akashic realm.

With great thanks and clarity I am now in the Akashic Record of my soul.

Now answer the following questions:

1. How does my body feel when I read this prayer?
2. Is there an emotional connection to this prayer? Do I feel it in my heart or gut?
3. What am I thinking? Where does my mind go?

4. Do I receive any images or pictures with this prayer?

How did that feel? The idea was for you to receive an intuitive feeling and a bit of information about the prayers. We will look at these prayers again and delve into the soul lineage of each prayer. Because every person is a unique individual and resonates with different vibrations and information than do other people, the prayers feel different for everyone. The Akashic Knowing School of Wisdom teaches multiple prayers in its classes to help students feel the vibration that is most compatible with them and their soul's lineage. New prayers are given from the Beings of Light as the energies of the students and the planet are upgraded in this beautiful time of shift.

You will be learning three of my students' favorite prayers to open your Record. Your unique lineage could be ancient or galactic, so what you might find is that one or two prayers resonate with you. Or maybe there's one you love, and another one that is useful when you want to work on asking more profound questions or you are ready to receive a detailed answer about your soul's path. You might find that one of the prayers will be good for short, concise answers, whereas another prayer is good for expansive heart space such as the energy long held in the goddess temples.

For myself, I find that one of the prayers is great for meditation because it's expansive and galactic. I love to just sit and meditate inside that prayer's energetic vibration. I suggest you experiment with all three of them. There is no right or wrong.

Working Inside of the Records

As I mentioned in the last chapter, it's not effective to memorize the prayers, because they are a vibrational key to unlock the door to your Record. You've learned about the prayers from outside of the Records and noticed how each prayer felt to you. In this chapter, you're going to receive more information about each prayer and learn which prayer resonates best with you and your soul lineage.

Whenever opening the Akashic Records, you are creating a sacred space where you are asking for assistance from the Akashic Beings of Light, whom we sometimes refer to as the Lords, Masters, and Teachers. They are all part of the Divine Source energy, the information arm of God. They live in the Divine Source vibration, and they wish to be of service to you by answering your questions and helping you in clearing and removing that which no longer serves you. You're acknowledging that the information is coming to you with clarity and ease, and that you're not channeling other people, other entities, or other beings. You are stating that you are in the Akashic Records specifically to do the work of the Divine.

Let's get started.

The Akashic Knowing Wisdom Prayer System

1. Set your intention.

It is vital to be clear and open to the wisdom and healing of the Akashic Records. Begin your time with the Akashic Records by setting your intention to be a pure and clear channel for yourself. The following prayer will assist you.

INTENTION FOR CLARITY PRAYER

Lords, Masters, and Teachers, please help me to remove what no longer serves me, including all hidden beliefs, prejudices, outdated patterns, programs, blocks, and constrictions, as I access Akashic Record information for myself today with clarity. I am here to do the work of the Divine. I am clear of other people's energy, and I am full of divine energy. Information moves freely to and through me.

2. **Choose one of the three prayers to work with.**

Recite the prayer out loud one time as it is written. Then *silently* repeat the prayer two times and insert your current legal name where **ME** or **MY** is written.

3. **Ask several questions related to your chosen topic.**

The more questions you ask, the deeper the answers will be and the broader the perspective you will receive from your Akashic Record.

4. **Fill yourself up with your highest energy.**

Use the following prayer.

PRAYER TO FILL UP WITH THE HIGHEST AKASHIC ENERGY

Please fill me up with my highest and best Akashic Record information and the highest and best physical-level energy and information I can now hold. Thank you for your healing today.

5. **When you are finished, close your Akashic Record using the Akashic Record Closing Prayer.**

AKASHIC RECORD CLOSING PRAYER

Thank you, dear Beings of Light, for the unconditional love, the wisdom, the information, and the healing I have received today.

Please help me to return fully into my complete human wholeness, in all dimensions, times, and planes. Please help me to integrate the information and healing received with ease and Grace.

*I ask that you close and lock the Records of **[Your Legal Name]** for now.*

So it is. Amen, Amen, Amen.

Opening Your Akashic Record

Are you ready? It is now time to go through the **Akashic Knowing Wisdom Prayer System** for opening your Akashic Record. The first few times you will be practicing opening and closing them. For your practice sessions, please use my questions. After you are used to working in the Akashic Records, you can then use your own questions. I will walk you through the process step by step.

We will now practice opening and closing the Akashic Records using each of the three Sacred Prayers my Beings of Light instructed me to share with you:

1. Akashic Record Prayer 1 (Sirius)

2. Akashic Record Prayer 2 (Arcturus)

3. Akashic Record Prayer 3 (Galactic Traveler)*

For this practice, you will open the first prayer and ask the questions listed following it. Then close that prayer using the Akashic Record Closing Prayer. Repeat the process for the second prayer, and the third. Record your answers in your journal.

*Note: These prayers are henceforth referred to simply as 1(S), 2(A), and 3(G) for simplicity.

AKASHIC RECORD PRAYER 1(S)

1. **Set your Intention, and then say the Intention for Clarity Prayer.**

INTENTION FOR CLARITY PRAYER

Lords, Masters, and Teachers, please help me to remove what no longer serves me, including all hidden beliefs, prejudices, outdated patterns, programs, blocks, and constrictions, as I access Akashic Record information for myself today with clarity. I am here to do the work of the Divine. I am clear of other people's energy, and I am full of divine energy. Information moves freely to and through me.

2. **Say Akashic Record Prayer 1(S).**

   Recite the prayer out loud one time as it is written, then *silently* repeat the prayer two times inserting your current legal name where **ME** or **MY** is written.

AKASHIC RECORD PRAYER 1(S)

*Divine Beings of Light of unconditional love, help me to center fully in this moment as I create this sacred space. Please wrap me in your love and allow me to travel to the highest realms of the Akasha available to **ME** today.*

*Lords, Beings of Light, and Teachers, I ask that you show me what it feels like to be a clear channel of **MY** Akashic Record.*

*Beings of Light, please guide me to the deepest Truth of **ME**. Support me in healing and releasing the appropriate karma and contracts that have brought me to this life. I give*

82

great thanks for your Divine Love, support, and protection on this journey.

After the Records are open: Feel the vibrational shift and say hello to the Beings of Light that have been keeping your Record for time immemorial.

3. **Ask several questions related to your chosen topic.** (For your practice sessions, ask the following questions.) When asking the following questions allow the information to flow through you by writing it in your journal.

   ✦ Please show me what it feels like to move out of my head and into my heart as I do this work today. (Notice how your body feels when you read this prayer. Take notes.)

   ✦ Akashic Masters, what is my emotional connection to this prayer? (Notice if you feel it in your heart or gut.)

   ✦ Is there a soul connection or past-life connection to this prayer? Please explain this to me.

   ✦ What is important for me to know today?

4. **Fill yourself up with your highest energy by saying the Fill Up Prayer.**

   PRAYER TO FILL UP WITH THE
   HIGHEST AKASHIC ENERGY

Please fill me up with my highest and best Akashic Record information and the highest and best physical-level energy and information I can now hold. Thank you for your healing today.

5. **Close and lock your Record by saying the Akashic Record Closing Prayer.**

AKASHIC RECORD CLOSING PRAYER

Thank you, dear Beings of Light, for the unconditional love, the wisdom, the information, and the healing I have received today.

Please help me to return fully into my complete human wholeness, in all dimensions, times, and planes. Please help me to integrate the information and healing received with ease and Grace.

I ask that you close and lock the Record of **ME**.

And so it is. Amen. Amen. Amen.

Here is an example of how you would silently say the prayer and insert your legal name at the **MY/ME**: "...Please wrap me in your love and allow me to travel to the highest realms of the Akasha available to **Mary Anne Smith** today.... Lords, Beings of Light, and Teachers, I ask that you show me what it feels like to be a clear channel of **Mary Anne Smith's** Akashic

Record...." Please notice that you are actually repeating the prayer three times: once out loud as you see it, and two times silently, with your legal name. You will do the same with the second prayer.

Each time you use the prayers, you raise your energetic vibration. The first time, you are stepping into the Akashic realm by opening the door to your Record; for the second and third time, you are moving into a greater depth of information in the Record of your soul, and your legal name is the key to unlocking your personal information. You will notice that in the Closing Prayer there is a sentence that states, "I ask that you close and lock the Record of [insert your legal name]." You always want to be sure that your Record is closed when you are finished.

You will be using the same system to open Akashic Prayer 2(A). If you're immediately continuing on with Prayer 2(A), please support your physical body and make sure you are fully grounded. Remember, this is a new, higher vibration than your body may be used to. I suggest that you move around a little, have a piece of chocolate, drink a glass of water, or do something else to make sure you are fully present and grounded in your body. Once you feel assured that you are, then use the **Akashic Knowing Wisdom Prayer System** for opening your Akashic Record. I have it all conveniently listed here so that you can go from one step to another without flipping pages.

Now open the second prayer and ask the questions listed following it. Then close that prayer using the Akashic Record Closing Prayer. Record your answers in your journal.

AKASHIC RECORD PRAYER 2(A)

1. **Set your Intention and then say the Intention Prayer.**

   INTENTION FOR CLARITY PRAYER

   Lords, Masters, and Teachers, please help me to remove what no longer serves me, including all hidden beliefs, prejudices, outdated patterns, programs, blocks, and constrictions, as I access Akashic Record information for myself today with clarity. I am here to do the work of the Divine. I am clear of other people's energy, and I am full of divine energy. Information moves freely to and through me.

2. **Say Akashic Record Prayer 2(A)**

   Recite the prayer out loud one time as it is written, then *silently* repeat the prayer two times, inserting your current legal name where **ME** or **MY** is written.

   AKASHIC RECORD PRAYER 2(A)

   *Akashic Lords, please help me to lay my multidimensional heart open to Divine love, as I lay down all resistance. I ask the Lords, Masters, and Teachers of **ME** to align me with you, in my Akashic Record.*

*Beings of Light of my Akashic Record, please show me the way to deepen into the Truth of **MY** soul.*

Please keep me safe and protected as I access Divine soul wisdom and information in my Akashic realm.

3. **Ask several questions related to your chosen topic.** (For your practice sessions, ask the following questions). When asking the following questions allow the information to flow through you onto a piece of paper.

   ✦ Please show me what it feels like to move out of my head and into my heart as I do this work today. (Notice how your body feels when you read this prayer. Take notes.)

   ✦ Akashic Masters, what is my emotional connection to this prayer? (Notice if you feel it in your heart or gut.)

   ✦ Is there a soul connection or past-life connection to this prayer? Please explain it to me.

   ✦ What is important for me to know today?

4. **Fill yourself up with your highest energy by saying the Fill Up prayer.**

   PRAYER TO FILL UP WITH THE
   HIGHEST AKASHIC ENERGY

Please fill me up with my highest and best Akashic Record information and the highest and best physical-level energy and information I can now hold. Thank you for your healing today.

5. **Close and lock your Record by saying the Akashic Record Closing Prayer.**

AKASHIC RECORD CLOSING PRAYER

Thank you, dear Beings of Light, for the unconditional love, the wisdom, the information, and the healing I have received today.

*Please help me to return fully into my complete human wholeness, in all dimensions, times, and planes. Please help me to integrate the information and healing received with ease and Grace. I ask that you close and lock the Record of **ME**. And so it is. Amen. Amen. Amen.*

AKASHIC RECORD PRAYER 3(G)

1. **Set your Intention and then say the Intention Prayer.**

INTENTION FOR CLARITY PRAYER

Lords, Masters, and Teachers, please help me to remove what no longer serves me, including all hidden beliefs, prejudices, outdated patterns, programs, blocks, and constrictions, as I access Akashic Record information for myself today with clarity. I am here to do the work of the Divine. I am clear of other people's energy, and I am full of divine energy. Information moves freely to and through me.

2. **Say Akashic Record Prayer 3(G).**

Recite the prayer out loud one time as it is written, then *silently* repeat the prayer two times, inserting your current legal name where **ME** or **MY** is written.

AKASHIC RECORD PRAYER 3(G)

*Divine Mother, Father, All that Is, please expand my state of consciousness and move **ME** into divine alignment with my Akashic Record.*

*I ask that the shields of protection be activated to encircle me as I move deeply into **MY** Akashic realm.*

*With great thanks and clarity I am now in the Akashic Record of **MY** soul.*

3. **Ask several questions related to your chosen topic.** (For your practice sessions, ask the following questions.) When asking the following questions allow the information to flow through you onto a piece of paper.

   ✦ Please show me what it feels like to move out of my head and into my heart as I do this work today. (Notice how your body feels when you read this prayer. Take notes.)

✦ Akashic Masters, what is my emotional connection to this prayer? (Notice if you feel it in your heart or gut.)

✦ Is there a soul connection or past-life connection to this prayer? Please explain it to me.

✦ What is important for me to know today?

4. **Fill yourself up with your highest energy by saying the Fill Up prayer.**

PRAYER TO FILL UP WITH THE HIGHEST AKASHIC ENERGY

Please fill me up with my highest and best Akashic Record information and the highest and best physical-level energy and information I can now hold. Thank you for your healing today.

5. **Close and lock your Record by saying the Akashic Record Closing Prayer.**

AKASHIC RECORD CLOSING PRAYER

Thank you, dear Beings of Light, for the unconditional love, the wisdom, the information, and the healing I have received today.

Please help me to return fully into my complete human wholeness, in all dimensions, times, and planes. Please help me to integrate *the information and healing received with ease and Grace. I ask that you close and lock the Record of **ME**. And so it is. Amen. Amen. Amen.*

You may find that you want to practice opening and closing your Record throughout a few days, or at least several hours. By doing so, you will be better able to discern which prayer feels best for you. Everyone is going to receive information differently. I suggest you journal your answers to each of the questions for each prayer so you can capture and record what's happening every time you open your Record. The records you keep will aid you in becoming aware of just how far you have come in time. Also, remember that you are building relationships between yourself and the Beings of Light.

You may actually receive a story about why you are emotionally connected to one of the prayers. It's not just, "Is there an emotional connection, yes or no?" Allow information in the form of pictures, feelings, stories, or past-life memories to come to you without judgment. When you start working in your Record, you will quickly discover that there are infinite possibilities for accessing information. That is part of the reason why so many people are interested in working within the Akashic Records realm. And what is even more beneficial is that the Beings of Light have made accessing the Records so much easier with these prayers.

Now that you have gone through working with prayers both outside and inside your Record, this is a good time to go back and re-read what you wrote about Prayer 1 when you were outside of the Record. Pay attention to the difference in the level of information you received intuitively compared to your journal entries when inside your Akashic Record. Did you notice any differences? If so, jot them down. I cannot emphasize enough the importance of taking copious notes when you are in the Records. You will gain so much validation from these processes, and the most important part about journaling is that patterns of behavior become evident, allowing for releasing them much more easily.

One area many of my students seem to comment on is how they feel after they close their Record. In the Akashic Record Closing Prayer, the word amen acts as an energetic lock. I like to picture myself turning three locks on a door. You may want to use that visual for yourself to ensure that you have indeed closed and locked your Record. A phenomenon I find common among new students is that now that they've finally entered their Records, many don't want to close them, so they don't really close and lock them. As a result, some questions I often hear are, "Why do I feel so tired?" "I thought I closed my Records, but I'm so exhausted." The truth is they didn't really close their Records; instead, they kept a foot in the door. When you first start to work in your Record, you may think that you fully closed it by reciting the closing prayer, but you actually didn't. Possibly you kept your foot in the door. Sometimes students will tell me, "But I keep hearing voices; I'm receiving information," and that is because they haven't really closed and locked their Records.

It will be beneficial for you if you get in the habit of saying, "I intend to close my Records. This is true. For now I am closing them in my etheric body, and I'm closing them in my heart. I have free entrance whenever I desire. It is safe to lock my Record." *Then* you can say the closing prayer, and literally visualize a door closing and three bolts locking—Amen, Amen, Amen. Many of us who love the vibration and have been waiting a lifetime to access it find it hard to lock the door; this is a gentle and loving way to leave your Record with the full understanding that you can return whenever you wish.

High vibration feels like physical exercise to some people, so I suggest you work in your Record every day for 20 to 30 minutes while you get in energetic shape, and then you can move into an hour in the Records or even many hours if you're working on a project such as writing a book or creating something.

As you continue on your Akashic Record journey while reading this book, you will learn healing prayers and other healing tools that you can utilize when in your Record. One thing that's important to learn now is that anytime you're working in your Record clearing out old energy, you need to replace it with new energy. Make sure you follow any such energy clearing with this prayer:

PRAYER TO FILL UP WITH THE HIGHEST AKASHIC ENERGY

Please fill me up with the highest and best Akashic Record information and the highest and best physical-level energy and information I can now hold.

Thank you for the healing today.

It's very important to replace the old energy you've released by filling yourself up with your highest and best Akashic Record information and physical-level energy. Nature abhors a vacuum, and when you release old blocked energy, there is an empty space that needs to be filled. Something will fill the newly cleared space, and you want it to be of a high vibrational energy that is in alignment with your soul.

Prayer Lineages

As I touched on briefly in the last chapter, each prayer represents a different soul lineage. Now I want to talk a little bit about these lineages.

About 100 years ago, when Edgar Cayce starting accessing the Akashic Field in a deep hypnotic trance, the Akashic energy began to come back to our planet. We are now aiding this resurgence by providing an easier structure through which people desiring this connection can access it. The energy of the Akasha has become more accessible through-out the years with the shift into the Age of Aquarius and the Harmonic Convergence, along with celestial alignments too numerous to name. Our recent step through the 2012 doorway to an energetic conscious-ness shift opened wide the call to access the Akashic Records.

When I was asked by the Lords of the Akashic Records to teach new prayers, they told me about the importance of multiple prayers. They explained that at this time in Earth's consciousness shift, many peo-ple would need to complete their connections to their lineages. Each one of the five prayers I teach in my Akashic Knowing Courses has a connection to a par-ticular planetary system: Arcturus, Sirius, Pleiades, Orion, and the Galactic Traveler. The three prayers you are learning in this book—Prayer 1(S), Prayer 2(A), and Prayer 3(G)—are the most popular with my students, and are also the ones the Beings of Light urged me to teach you, and I think you will find learning their history quite intriguing. You may even have a feeling deep inside you when reading about each prayer. Their story may ignite an ancient flame buried deep within your soul.

Prayer 1(S) is connected to Sirius, the "Dog Star." Sirius is where the ancient Egyptian Gods originated. When I clairvoyantly look at that star world, I re-member many lifetimes in which I lived on the planet Sirius. I recall lifetimes when I was part of the ancient Egyptian god lineage of Isis and Osiris. The Beings of Light told me that the Egyptian gods came to Earth

95

on a journey of exploration. They were beings who were literally much larger than life, who appeared to humanity at the time as gods. At first, they continued to come to earth, accepting and acting out the god's role. Eventually they decided that they wanted to stay on this planet as humanity evolved, so they became embodied as humans. Because of their massive size, those beings who chose to, fragmented into hundreds of smaller souls and were then born into the gods of the Isis and Osiris temples.

As a result, many of us here on Earth have the lineage of Isis or Osiris, or one of the lesser-known gods. Many people will find that in their own Akashic Record, or sometimes during an intuitive reading or psychic reading, someone will say, "Oh, you are Isis. You are of the Isis lineage." Historically, that would mean that you originated from the star system Sirius, and that you were part of the shift from the great mother Isis and father Osiris into a human body. You are part of their fragments, which were embodied by human babies. In time, their lineage has grown as thousands of human Isises and Osirises gave birth. If someone tells you that you are Isis energy or of the Isis lineage, that does not necessarily mean that you, yourself, were Isis, but you may have been one of the thousand original beings who embodied here at some point in ancient history, or one born into that genetic lineage. As you learn to navigate within your Record, ask the Beings of Light to share the ancient knowledge of Sirius.

Prayer 2(A) is connected to Arcturus. There haven't been a lot of Arcturians coming to Earth in the last few thousand years, but what I am noticing is that quite a few are here now with a particular type of mission. The information that I have received in the Galactic Records about Arcturus is that the Arcturians were a warring people for a very long time, and then they changed their ways. They became awakened as a people and as a planet, and they stopped fighting. My experience with students who resonate with this prayer is that they feel a lack of trust in this life, and they are driven toward heartfelt work. It is as though they are here to heal the heart energies through trust of others.

Arcturians began to consider the galaxies around them, and the consequences of their warring ways. They realized that their old ways were about to kill their planet and other neighboring planets. The only way Arcturians thought they could stop the wars was to isolate themselves by separating from anyone not living on Arcturus. What they did was wall themselves off on their home planet of Arcturus. They gave up their interplanetary travel to focus on Divine love and unity, and by doing so they became blissful, awakened beings living within their walled cities. They are an interesting group because they have big, tender hearts, but they often have old walls of protection around them. In ancient times, protecting their hearts served them well as it kept them safe from retaliation from their warring neighbors. In the present time, they are here to open their hearts to humanity.

The greatest challenge is sharing their loving hearts with humanity, and communicating wisdom about seeking unconditional love and forgiveness. Do you understand how your greatest challenge in life may be because of isolation and shutting down to love?

One of the reasons there are quite a few Arcturians coming to Earth at this time is that they want to assist us in our transition. They transitioned from a warring, conquering people to a completely peaceful, awakened people. This is similar to what we are going through here on Earth. We are moving in the direction of change from wars, conquering, and suppressing groups of people, to being connected in an awakened state of being. A lot of Arcturian souls are coming to work in the Akashic Records. I am sure that anyone who resonates with Prayer 2(A) has lived on Arcturus. How about you? You can often recognize an Arcturian because they are here teaching us how to live in our hearts, to become awakened and enlightened, all the while continuing to live an embodied human life here on planet Earth. They are teaching us that enlightenment does not have to mean that we leave, ascend, or die. Nor do we need to go live in a monastery, cloister ourselves from civilization, or spend our time on Earth constantly meditating. Our next step is to create a heavenly and blissful life here on Earth and to enjoy the gifts of Mother Earth.

I call **Prayer 3(G)** the Galactic Traveler. It is not associated with any one planet, plane, or dimension as are the other two, but denotes a soul that delights in traveling and experiencing much of what the galaxies have to offer. These souls particularly enjoy experiencing different perspectives and the expansiveness in the Universe. They have traveled to many planets and galaxies and feel at home in many places. Many times these souls are also known as "Star Seeds" and may have come with soul contracts to bring new or otherworldly technology and information here to Earth at this time.

There are also numerous planets where we have not lived, so the prayers connected to those soul lineages may not resonate with you. I want to ask you not to form any judgments about your personal lineage. All the planets and galaxies were home to powerful and wise beings, and there are many more places I do not have prayers for as of yet. When the Beings of Light feel it is time, I trust they will give them to me.

The Pleiades, also known as the Seven Sisters, are where the Mayans are believed to have traveled from. These ancient beings have held so much informational energy for planet Earth because they were very close to our planet. Of course, all of the planets presented numerous skills, talents, intelligence, and creative knowledge to our planet. The Sirians and the Egyptians were powerful builders and bringers of technology to our planet, whereas the Arcturians, with their heart-centered energies, are helping to awaken humanity and the Earth to unconditional love. The Galactic Travelers possess many talents to share with our planet's inhabitants. When I started studying the Akashic Records, the Pleadian prayer was the only prayer I knew about. The Beings of Light told me that I would open my own Akashic Records school, and that I would receive from the Galactic Records multiple prayers that would resonate with many more people. I was told the new prayers would make accessing the information easier. Bringing forth these prayers is a beautiful and profound experience for me. I am so grateful to the Lords of the Akashic Field for gifting me with the responsibility of bringing them forward and teaching them to you now.

The Beings of Light have said it is time for wisdom and Divine guidance to come back to humanity with ease. Your personal Akashic guidance supports you in creating your soul's desire and helping you to actualize your life purpose—and to create heaven on Earth as we move into the fifth dimension.

The Beings of Light have shared with us that the Akashic Records also provide their own path to awakening. Working in the Records enables us to shift from our small human view to the divine expanse and awareness of all, because we are in Divine Source energy. When we are in this high vibrational frequency, we are accessing the Divine mind and the wisdom of the past, present, and future. When we spend a lot of time in our own Record, we shift our perspective from the dense, worldly view to the perspective of Divine wisdom. When we actively meditate in this vibration, our awareness of who we truly are as divine beings supports our awakening process at a conscious level.

As you open your heart and expand your mind, the Beings of Light will help you to connect to the divinity of which we are all One. It is truly its own path to awakening, and a magnificent journey back to the truth of who we have always been.

Journaling: Pages of Self-Healing

A journal is a powerful tool to help you evoke personal change. It will allow you to recognize your potential for personal and spiritual growth.

Here are a few reasons for you to journal:

✦ You will find that you will receive a tremendous amount of information while working in your Record, and it is difficult to remember it all. You may not completely understand all of the information in the moment, and having a written document and the ability to revisit the information will enable you to receive an even more in-depth meaning.

✦ Journaling allows you to look for central or recurring themes. Identify strong messages to bring them into awareness for expansion or completion. If you keep reliving the same situation, you can go back to your journal to find a similar situation. Without journaling and having a record of questions and information, you may not find similarities in different occurrences. But in going back to your journal, you could find a trigger or button that is pushed every time you run into that situation. Now you can find it and ask for more information in the Records to find out if there is something you have been overlooking in these scenarios. Possibly you have a soul contract or karma that you're ready to complete but have not yet released.

✦ You can discover who you really are by recording and rereading your experiences. Journaling will help clarify what you believe, what you want to do with your life, and how to go about creating that life with support from the Beings of Light.

✦ Reading over your journals is quite validating. They remind you of how much you've grown, what you have overcome, and also what you need to do to stay in alignment with your intentions.

✦ Journaling while in your Record creates your own personal link to the Divine Source. You are writing an inspirational guidebook for those who follow after you.

It's always amazing to me when I look back at my journals after a month, and most especially after a year or more. I can go back and remember what I was asking about, or what seemed so challenging in that moment, which is now in the distant past. It feels so validating to see my journey and how much help

I received from the Akashic guidance. It reminds me of how supported I am as I make my way through challenging times, which always leads to expansive moments. Journaling helps to remind us how far we've come, and elevates the work we are doing and have done. It helps to show us that when we pay attention to the guidance and the wisdom that we receive in our Akashic Record, our lives do become so much easier. The Records can help us alter our course, and change our lives for the better. This is profound work, and I feel that it is productive to acknowledge the courage to go inward to move ourselves forward every day in loving guidance.

It is also important that we do not feel as though we are just doing something we have to do. The thought that we *have* to open the Records to ask questions and seek guidance negates the wisdom and unconditional love the Beings of Light hold for us. When we validate ourselves by seeing how far we have come on this journey called life, and how everything in our lives has changed for the better, it inspires us to do it even more.

At one point, I had bought a new bookshelf and starting rearranging my books and journals. I had all of my Akashic journals stacked into a big pile on the floor, and they all fell over. There were quite a few of them because I had been writing in my journal for many years. As I walked through my room, I just stepped over the pile of them. Years earlier the Beings of Light had told me that there were a few books for me to write, and I got stuck on linear thinking. *What am I supposed to write? What am I supposed to say?* And as I stepped over all these journals that day, I heard a voice in my head telling me I'd just stepped over "the books." I heard these words: "Look through them. Reread them, and when you do, you will be filled with wisdom and information that you can share and write about." So, you never know when your journals will become useful for you on your life path.

Am I Really in My Akashic Record?

When we first start accessing our Akashic Record, there is often a part of us that doubts that we are really hearing or feeling what we are hearing or feeling. Sometimes, we feel that we aren't clairvoyant enough because we don't see a lot of pictures. We may think the voice we hear sounds like our own voice, which leads us to think that it can't be the Beings of Light of our Record; maybe it's our egos getting involved by giving us a lot of advice. Here are some tips you can use to work through the doubts and move into trust.

✦ If you've had a busy or stressful day and then attempt to open your Record, you may be filled with other people's energy or energy from the day. Take time to calm and center yourself first. Do a short meditation such as Guided, Guarded, and Protected, which we did earlier in the book. (Guided, Guarded, and Protected is also available as

104

an audio meditation with music on *www. theinfinitewisdom.com/goldenegg.*)

+ Another helpful tool is to recite the Prayer to Clear Others' Energy, given in the next chapter. This prayer, as well as many other helpful tools, help you to move everyone's energy out of your space so that you can be centered in your own truth.

+ Whenever you doubt whether you are in your Record, the simplest thing to do is close your Record, become centered and grounded in your body, and then start over. Go through the **Akashic Knowing Wisdom Prayer System** again. Remember to always read and focus on the words of the prayer as you open your Record. Do not memorize the opening prayer. The Intention for Clarity Prayer is particularly beneficial when your doubt is very strong.

+ Focusing your questions on one subject can be useful in receiving a bigger picture so you can feel the depth of the answers. This process will help to relieve doubt. When you think, *I wouldn't have thought of that*, then you can be assured the answer isn't coming from you, but instead is divinely guided.

+ Start with simple questions that aren't life-changing. As with all new tools, you need to practice using them to become proficient in wielding them. An example of a simple question is, "Is there a physical exercise or food that would be beneficial for me today?" Not, "What is my life purpose?" or "Should I get a divorce and sell the house?"

✦ You may wish to ask your questions in a different way, or ask the Beings of Light to assist in formulating new questions.

✦ If you find that you are still not receiving any information, then there may be an interference pattern you need to break. In order to receive the answer to your question, you can easily release the pattern of interference by asking the Beings of Light to guide you to one or more of the healing prayers I give you in Chapter 3. Repeat the healing prayer as many times as feels appropriate, and then ask, "Has the interference been lifted?" If not, repeat the prayer until the information starts to flow again.

✦ It is helpful to set and clear your prayer space by reciting all five healing prayers from Chapter 3 before opening your Akashic Record.

✦ Use your Energy Release Grace Point, discussed in Chapter 3, to redirect the conscious mind to access the information you are seeking. This also releases constrictions in your energy field to make accessing the information easier.

✦ Pay close attention to how the answers feel in your body. Do they give you goose bumps or bring tears to your eyes? They might just feel energetically resonant, aligning with your heart, no matter whether you believe the words or not. Write your experience down and reread it later.

✦ Move out of your head by writing the question down in your journal and then letting the answers flow through you. Don't pay attention to what you're "getting" as you write; just wait until you are finished receiving the information. When you go back to reread what you had received, you may be surprised by the information.

Learning to Trust

Let's play with what you've learned so far by doing another exercise that will show you the difference in information between what you have received outside of your Record and what you have received inside it.

First, ask yourself, "What can I do to bring more peace and joy to myself and into my life?"

Take maybe three or four minutes to answer that question *outside* of your Record. If you remember, being outside of your Record means using your intuition, in your non-magical way of being—in your Muggle state, if you're a Harry Potter fan! Write down your answers, including any feelings you may have.

Next, *open* your Record using the prayer that res-onates best with you. Go ahead and say that prayer once out loud and two times silently with your legal name in place of the "**me**" or the "**my**." Now, with your Record open, ask, "What can I do to bring more peace and joy to myself and into my life?" Again, write down your question and answer and remember to get out of your head and just let the energy flow. Write in your journal whatever you are thinking or feeling, or whatever that voice in your head is saying, even if it's coming across more as a picture.

Read the two answers out loud or to yourself. Did you notice the difference in the energy outside of the Record versus inside the Record? Did you have an "aha!" moment after reading what you wrote down? Sometimes, when we ask a question both outside and inside our Record, we receive completely different information. Outside your Record you may think, "I need to get more exercise," but when you open the Record of your soul, the Beings of Light are talking about how to expand more into joy by being more spiritually centered, using meditation, or taking a walk in nature.

Also, be aware that the information can show up as an inkling of something different, or, for some of you, it may come through as a specific suggestion. For example, you may think you need to spend more time working in your Record to bring more joy into your life. The Beings of Light will tell you some-thing similar, guiding you to a specific meditation or to a specific prayer, or to a Zen Buddhist walking meditation to quiet your mind.

Keep practicing as much as you possibly can. Use the Records to help you in making even the smallest daily decisions. Practicing inside and outside of your Record is a fabulous way to become strong and to validate the information you receive. For example, ask yourself, "What would be beneficial for me to have for dinner tonight?" Write down whatever comes into your mind. Then open your Akashic Record to ask the Beings of Light what you should have for dinner tonight that would be beneficial for your body, and compare what you receive.

Finally, don't be surprised if at some point you open your Record and receive a substantial download of information about who you are as a soul, where you have been in past lives, what you have done in those lives, and what you have come here to do in this lifetime. For some, this happens early on in the process; for others, it happens after a year, or during their advanced Akashic Records studies.

Chapter 3

Healing Through
the Akashic Records

Clearing Issues with Akashic Support

The Akashic Records are an umbrella of information that contain infinite wisdom and Divine Source energy. It is the highest energetic vibration we can access. All you have to do to gain healing from the Akashic field of energy is open your Record and allow the energy to enfold you. Please take this to heart, and ask your Beings of Light to assist you in clearing and releasing old energetic patterns that no longer serve you.

Remember when you were in 1st grade and 2nd grade, learning to read? It's the same with learning to use the Akashic Record for information and healing. It takes time, focus, and attention to learn to work in the different areas within your Record.

The Beings of Light have provided us with tools that are profound, yet simple to use. I must advise you to not be fooled by their simplicity. They are powerful. In this chapter, I have included five healing prayers and a variety of guided visualizations for you to use while you are working with the Beings of Light in your Akashic Record. You can memorize these prayers, you may use them inside your Record, or you may use them at any time during the day when your Record is closed. I suggest that you print them out, carry them with you, and offer them to friends in need of clearing. The five prayers you will find in the following pages are:

1. The Forgiveness Prayer
2. The Prayer for Physical Clearing
3. The Prayer for Clearing Others' Energies
4. The Prayer for Clearing Entities and Energy Patterns
5. The Prayer for Aligning with Your Soul

The Beings of Light gave humanity these healing tools with love. They wanted to help us remove mental and emotional blocks from our past, so that we can move forward with ease, love, and grace.

Calling Back Your Energy

We leave our energy scattered around the world without even realizing it. For example, when we travel to a beautiful place, we often leave reluctantly, and the part of us that wants to stay inadvertently leaves a piece of ourselves behind. We leave that energy behind to sustain a connection. When we talk on the phone with our friends and family, then go to meetings and work, we leave parts of our energy behind with each meaningful encounter. When we have had a fabulous time at a gathering, continuing to think about it, remembering, or reminiscing leaves bits of us behind. We might even leave a piece of our energy behind if we've had a heated discussion or argument with somebody, just by continuing to be upset or angry. When you imagine the cumulative effect of leaving small pieces of your energy scattered about throughout a lifetime, you can see how it can be very draining.

Sometimes, we can actually feel people in different areas of our body. For instance, the telepathic channels around your eyes coincide with your sinuses. You may think you're stuffy from the weather change, but in fact, it may be because someone is thinking about you and having a conversation in their head with you. You might be surprised how often you unconsciously leave your energy connected to other people and places. It can cause a feeling of fragmentation. As if you are not quite whole. You can't quite put your finger on it but you are not 100-percent present.

One of the most powerful tools I offer my students is guided visualizations that help them call back their own energy. So let's get started on reclaiming and drawing back your energy. You will feel wonderfully full of yourself—in a good way, of course.

CALLING BACK YOUR ENERGY MEDITATION

You will start with the breath. Take three deep breaths. For the first one, fill your whole body from the tips of your toes all the way up to the top of your head. Exhale deeply and completely. For your second breath, fill your belly until it expands fully, hold it for a moment, and then exhale slowly. Your third breath will be focused in your heart area as you allow your heart to open and expand to breathe in peace and joy. Exhale to release anything that no longer serves you in that moment, or stops you from experiencing the peace and joy you just breathed into your heart.

Next, soften your eyes as you let your body relax into your chair. Invite your spirit to come fully down into your physical body. Feel the divine support all around you as you connect to dear Mother Earth beneath your feet. Thank the Earth for supporting you as you walk on her, each and every day, as you go forward on your journey.

It's grounding if you can go outside and walk barefoot on the grass or on the sand at the beach.

Wherever you live, connect to and enjoy the earth beneath your feet, and ask to feel the earth energy running up through your feet and into your body.

What you are going to do now is to imagine there is a big golden sun about the size of a basketball above your head. Set the intention that as the golden sun is spinning and spinning, it is calling back your very own energy—all the energy that you have left scattered around the world. Imagine this golden sphere continuing to spin above your head. It is above your crown chakra, and it is calling back all of your positive and loving energy that you had scattered and left behind. That energy is melting and merging with that golden sun. Take a moment and notice what you see or feel.

Continue to let the big golden ball spin and spin and spin, breathing deeply, feeling or seeing that energy coming back into the golden ball of sun. The golden sun is calling back your energy as though it is a magnet. As the energy magnetizes to the sun, it turns into beautiful, golden, liquid sunlight, and this liquid sunlight pours down into your crown chakra. As your energy comes back, it is converted into the highest and best gold vibration of you, returning home into your body, into your energy field, into your auric field. It returns to wherever it came from, it returns to the highest and best place for it to go; you do not have to figure out where. Now see the sun's spin slowing down as all of your energy that is available now has returned. See that beautiful golden sun turning into a ball of liquid golden light.

The golden ball melts right down into your body, and maybe you can feel the warmth dripping through your body; you may notice the energy as a tingle running all the way down into your toes. It is the highest energy of you returning home to you now.

Karma and Forgiveness: The Forgiveness Prayer

In this section, I'll share with you the Forgiveness Prayer that assists in clearing karma. This prayer was given by the Akashic Records' Beings of Light to aid humanity in releasing old karmic energy that is holding them back from completing their souls' purpose.

First, though, I wish to explain how the Beings of Light speak of karma. I feel it's important to be clear about what karma is and is not. It is not a punishment; it is not an eye for an eye or a tooth for a tooth. Karma is the completion of a cycle of growth. As souls we come to experience all aspects of life on Earth. When we leave the chosen endeavor for whatever reason, karma is created by that incomplete action. In other words, we haven't learned what we came to learn or grown as a soul in the way we had intended.

Picture each lifetime as a pie. You're going along in life, nourishing your soul by eating the pie, when something occurs that upsets you. It's so upsetting that you jump out of that story; you walk away from the pie. So there you are, leaving two-thirds of the pie unfinished, uneaten. We do this in numerous ways. Sometimes, we do it by dying. At times, people are so miserable in their lives that their bodies say, "Okay, this is no good; let's leave. We can come back and try again in another life." People find themselves very ill, so they let go. Or we have an accident and die. Sometimes we turn to drugs or alcohol to numb our pain—in this case, we haven't left physically, but we've left emotionally. Those are just a few examples of how people can escape their karma and leave the remaining pie, unfinished.

In addition, each person is given a couple of chances to leave their life—their pie—if they choose. I call these "jumping-off points." You might have up to five or six different points in life where there is a place to jump out of the lifetime. You might have a terrible accident in which you miraculously walk away unscathed—that could have been a jumping-off point for you, but your soul chose not to leave. If your soul was miserable, deciding that this life was not working, that an uncorrectable mistake was made, then your soul may decide to use that "accident" to leave. Remember, all of those soul choices are usually going on unconsciously. When someone does not leave after those accidents, it is because the soul feels as though it has that life under control. It's as if the soul says, "I know what I am doing. Things may or may not look perfect on the outside, but I am on my path. I am making my way. I am clearing my karma. I am doing my work." The person walks away from a serious accident unscathed, or with minor bumps and bruises, but somehow changed.

Because we are unique souls, there are infinite possibilities for how we as people, and we as souls, will react. For example, there is the person who experiences great bodily harm from an accident, and then goes on to be a role model because of the hardships he overcame and the wisdom he can now bring to humanity. Another option is also possible. There is the person who has what we would call a minor accident, and then dies for no obvious reason. That accident was likely a jumping-off point. Incidents such as this may happen because we have come to finish a lot of karma from another lifetime, but when it shows up in this life we do not know how to deal with it, so we leave the story. We jump away from that pie by dying.

We leave the story of our life in so many other ways, too. As a soul, before we come into a body, we often choose to complete karma from a past life. We create a soul contract with a soul we had a complex relationship with in a past life. In this life, the soul's desire is to finish the old karma by supporting our partner. When the relationship becomes complicated again in this life, we abandon our partner and leave a mess behind. It might be a traumatic divorce, or, in a business partnership, suing the business partner for all rights to the business information. When we do this we do not complete that karma, as we have not forgiven our partners. We are very angry and are holding grudges. Instead of finishing our karma with that person, we have created new karma because we left with anger, disappointment, and emotional drama in our wake. We may even have harmed people physically or financially. Because we are having a human experience in the dense energy of anger, fear, guilt, or pride, we have not been able to move into a place of forgiveness. The good news is that karma is with our *selves*, or souls, and it is something we can clear through forgiveness and unconditional love.

Another example of jumping away from the pie and creating karma is when we leave through addiction, such as alcoholism or drug addiction. Those are ways to leave, just not physically. We may stick around, we may let the body hang out, and we may appear to be functioning as we stay in the marriage, relationship, or partnership, but the truth is we have left energetically, which is a form of abandonment. We have become an addict, whether of a substance or of anger or of some abusive trait, and we are not present mentally or emotionally. We are harming ourselves and others, and there will be a time when our soul decides to complete that karma and learn and grow in the way it had originally intended.

Those are a few examples of how we can create karma in our lives. In order for us to complete our story, we have to finish the whole pie. In doing so, we grow spiritually. It is important to be aware of what your karma is and to complete it. This is one of the soul contracts our spirit chooses when we incarnate. If we don't complete the karma by giving and receiving love and forgiveness in our current lifetime, then we will have other opportunities to complete the karma in another lifetime within similar situations or patterns. So look for patterns in your life, and seek to find the karma so that it can be completed once and for all. When you move into the vibration of unconditional love, you have completed the circle and have released that karma. One way to know if you have achieved a karmic release is to take note of your thoughts and emotions regarding that person. When she has safe passage through your mind and heart, your work with her is done. Ask yourself if you can think of her and feel unattached to her words or actions. If the answer is yes, there are no longer any emotional upsets or traumatic stories that arise when you think of her.

Of course, it doesn't mean that you have to stay in a relationship with that person, nor does it mean you're going to stay in an abusive relationship or allow your children to be subjected to an abusive family member. But you can forgive others on a soul level, and even on a personality level, if it's appropriate. You can say to yourself, "I see the truth of who you are as a divine soul just like me, and I forgive the soul that you are." I strongly encourage you to move into a place of forgiveness for yourself and the other person or persons by using the following Forgiveness Prayer given to me by the Beings of Light.

Forgiveness is the quickest and simplest way to clear karma throughout time and space. It allows us to heal our past, which consists of anything we may have done to others or ourselves prior to this moment. This includes our childhoods and our past lives. The Forgiveness Prayer is a subtle but extremely powerful prayer that helps to clear all the negativity that builds within and around us. Working with this prayer consecutively for 33 days heals the pain and separation we experience in negative and painful relationships with God/Spirit/Source, and other people or situations in our lives.

Whenever you recite this prayer, allow yourself to breathe deeply and slowly, moving into your heart.

THE FORGIVENESS PRAYER

Divine, Spirit, Source, please move me into a state of forgiveness toward anyone or anything that has hurt me, consciously or unconsciously, from the beginning of time to this present moment. I now forgive them as I release the energy of the past.

Divine, Spirit, Source, please move me into a state of forgiveness toward myself for any hurt that I have caused others, consciously or unconsciously, from the beginning of time to this present moment. I now forgive myself and I release the energy of the past.

Divine, Spirit, Source, please move me into a state of forgiveness toward myself for any hurt that I have caused myself, consciously or unconsciously, from the beginning of time to this present moment. I now forgive myself and release the energy of the past.

I invoke the power of Grace and forgiveness to transform my body, mind, and heart, as I return to my divine innocence. And so it is.

Allow yourself to continue breathing slowly and deeply, as you perceive, see, and feel the old karmic energy as it is uplifted. Repeat the prayer two more times or until you feel the process has been completed.

One of the beautiful things about this prayer, and the other Akashic Records healing prayers, is that you do not need to know the specifics. You do not need to name a person, or have to remember or relive the situation. You can clear the karma from a past life without remembering that lifetime.

I often tell the story about how I used to feel as though I was an awful mother. I had three babies in a very short amount of time. My son was 1 1/2 at the time my twins were born, so I had three babies under the age of 2 years old, and all three were in diapers. The first eight years were challenging for me, and I often felt as though I was this terrible mother, even though I was home all day long with them. I was always trying to be the greatest mother I could ever be, but the feeling that I was not doing a very good job never left me. My friends would look at me and say, "I don't get it, why do you think you are a bad mother? How could you possibly imagine that? You do everything for and with your kids." I didn't know where that feeling was coming from until I started to work on it in my Akashic Record. The Beings of Light meet us where we are, so we have to ask a question before we can receive an answer. I had to ask them specifically, "Why do I feel like a bad mother? Is there something I had done? Is there some old karma or something that I am trying to complete as a mother?" When I asked those questions, I received a clear picture of a past life in which one of my children was born malformed and sick. In the world at that time, we could not keep handicapped children. It was in a small village thousands of years ago, at a time when parents would leave those children out in the forest or mountains overnight to die of the cold or be eaten by wild animals. And that's what happened to my baby in that past life. I realized that the pain and guilt about being a terrible mother wasn't even from this lifetime. Once I understood its roots, the realization lifted a portion of the burden. I used the Forgiveness Prayer for 60 days to make sure that I fully and completely forgave myself for allowing my baby to die in that lifetime.

Frequently, we will notice there are many lifetimes strung together that are causing the emotional pain. In my case, there were additional lifetimes when my children had starved to death or otherwise died from illness. People used to have so many children because only about half of them would make it through the winters, influenza, diseases, and starvation. I lived many of those types of lives, as I'm sure many of you did also. This is the truth of who we are, and who we have been, because we are infinite beings who have been around for hundreds and hundreds of lifetimes. We have experienced it all, and not just once. We are not bad people, if our child accidentally dies; it is an experience that our soul, and the soul of the child, chose, for a multitude of reasons. Sometimes the soul decides to come in and live a very short life. Often, it is a new soul that is just learning how to navigate life in a physical body. That soul may decide to be stillborn, or to live for only a day or two. Another example is when the soul decides to have a lifetime in which the body is handicapped in some way, so that the soul can figure out how to navigate living in a physical form with help from caregivers throughout that life.

The Forgiveness Prayer is a profound prayer for working with clearing and releasing karma and trauma in matters of the heart. This prayer clears karma throughout time and space, allowing us to heal anything prior to this moment. For example, if you had an argument with someone, then felt bad about it, you could forgive yourself and the other person for any karma created by the argument, whether it was yesterday or 20 years ago. Forgiveness is always effective. When we don't forgive, our energy can become blocked, holding us back from making great strides forward in our lives.

Feeling Blocked: The Prayer for Physical Clearing

The next Akashic prayer assists in releasing the energies that affect you on a physical level. This is a great prayer to use when you are feeling blocked for no known reason, and using the Forgiveness Prayer didn't clear the energy. As with all of these prayers, you can use this one inside or outside of your Akashic Record. If you're at work and feeling a little stuck, or a little sad, reciting the Forgiveness Prayer and the Clearing Prayer would be helpful. When you begin accessing your personal Akashic Record, it is quite useful to use the Forgiveness Prayer and the Physical Clearing Prayer so that you can be sure that you are clear of negative energies. Pay special attention to what you are feeling before reciting the prayers, so that you know how they affect you over time.

THE PRAYER FOR PHYSICAL CLEARING

Divine Mother, Father, Goddess, God, and Beings of Light of my Akashic Record, please hold me and support me as I open to receive healing and clearing on multidimensional levels. Please remove any blockage that no longer serves me from any time, place, or dimension. Please upgrade my physical and etheric bodies so that I can hold more light with ease. Please unchain, unconstrain, clear, and open my multidimensional heart on all planes and dimensions. Please move me into a state of forgiveness throughout time

and space, clearing all connected karma. I give
great thanks for your divine love, wisdom, and
grace. Amen.

Creating Boundaries: The Prayer for Clearing Others' Energies

This prayer is a helpful tool when you feel other people's energy in your space. For example, think of a time when you got a headache, sinus attack, or a backache all of a sudden. When those physical discomforts show up after having a conversation with someone, you have merged their energy with yours, and it's now affecting you adversely. This is not a judgment about the person or his or her energy; we are usually more clairsentient than we realize and often wish to be of service to others by taking on their physical or emotional pain.

The clearer your energy field is, the more you are able feel others in your space. So the next time you feel uncomfortable after being around other people, know it most likely isn't your stuff and that you picked up someone else's energy. So do carry the prayer with you and use it multiple times throughout the day. Remember that the more you work in your Akashic Record, the clearer your energy will become, which allows you to detect when someone is in your energy field.

The Prayer to Clear Others' Energies, given in the following paragraph, can be used whenever you feel any type of sensation that may come from someone other than yourself. It can be physical, emotional, or mental—or all three. It really depends on the encounter you were involved in with other people. For example, we can absorb other people's energy empathically, because, by nature, human beings are empathic. We can often quite innocently do it in an effort to understand other people, or to help them with their pain or challenges. People come into our energy field to understand us, to receive physical energy, or, sometimes, just to communicate with us. Often, this unconscious act is not a good one for us, because we inadvertently allow others to fill our energy field. It is hard enough for us to find our soul's path without having someone else's energy interfering with our process of spiritual growth. So to clear out other people's energy from your field, you can do this prayer multiple times throughout the day. Try it at least two or three times a day while you are clearing your energy field.

THE PRAYER FOR CLEARING OTHERS' ENERGIES

Mother, Father, Goddess, God, please assist me in clearing and releasing all outside energies that are in my body, aura, and energy field. Please send them back to the person from whom they came. Or send them to the Divine Source to be recycled for the highest good of all. I am filled with my purest energy and the highest vibration I can now hold.

Clearing Disembodied Souls: The Prayer for Clearing Entities and Energy Patterns

This prayer clears entities and energy patterns. There are many disembodied souls, also called ghosts, on Earth at this time who wish to return to the Light. They can be people who passed away suddenly, who weren't ready to go, possibly through a traumatic accident. And even though they are dead, they didn't disengage with their human body. So they continue to walk around on the Earth plane, unaware that they have died, thinking they are still alive. They have lost their way and become trapped here, some for a long time. Very often they are trying to complete any karma that was created relating to their death. Because that isn't possible, it becomes important for them to return to the Light to allow for full manifestation of their soul. Remember the pie scenario that I used to explain karma? Disembodied souls are another perfect example of leaving the earth plane with an unfinished pie.

There are many other types of entities and energies visiting our earth plane. Some are extraterrestrials, from other dimensions, visiting here. It's easier for them to ride along in your energy field than to incarnate and begin the whole cycle of life here on Earth. Others may reside in the fairy, or elemental realms, who want information about humanity, possibly to help us or maybe just to learn and grow on their own soul path. No matter what we call them, or what plane, planet, or dimension they are from, they are always part of Source, and their souls are also on a journey. They are doing what souls do, experiencing and learning new things. We, as souls, are all growing throughout infinite time and space.

In rare cases, souls can be sent to a secluded space, sometimes referred to as a jail, where cosmic police guard them. This happens when a person has reacted with extreme violence to others; therefore, he or she needs to be detained until the soul can come into alignment with the universal laws of Light. Souls such as those of Hitler and Jeffrey Dahmer have become twisted in darkness for various reasons, so those souls are held in a place where they cannot cause any more harm to others. Sometimes we have contacts with dark entities that want to gain power over us or over our situations in life. There are many different stories about what a dark entity or energy pattern is, but often the dark energies come to us specifically because we have an old past-life contract with them. You may have had a past life in the 1600s in which you came to help the Earth, but there was so little light to access on the planet at that time that you contracted with the darker forces to boost your energy so you could connect with your magical powers. You vowed to always support this entity and now it's back to have its debt paid in full so it can gain some of its old power again. You can now finish and clear these old contracts in your Akashic Record.

Random energy patterns can appear to be ghosts, but they are actually old residual energy patterns that have not left—most of the soul is gone but pieces of that energy pattern are still around. You can send that residual energy to the light by using the following prayer. We can also notice patterns of energy that we have created over time. Have you ever experienced a "stuck in a rut" feeling? Well, that may be an energy pattern, and by using the next prayer daily the pattern will loosen its hold. Furthermore, if you or anyone you know finds an energy that feels dark, creepy, or spooky, it may be attached to the house you live in, or the land surrounding the house. The Prayer for Clearing Entities and Energy Patterns is profound for this. Use it to clear entities and energy patterns for yourself or for someone else who asks for help. Be sure to have the intention that any outside influences, entities, beings, or energy patterns in our space, energy field, or house that do not belong must leave—now—never to return. Recite this prayer with that specific desire in mind. Remember, intention is very important when working on clearing, for yourself or for anyone else.

THE PRAYER FOR CLEARING ENTITIES AND ENERGY PATTERNS

I call upon Archangel Michael and his legions alongside the Akashic Beings of Light and the Divine Source. Please surround me with your light and love and keep me protected and safe as I command the release of all energies, interferences, thoughts, feelings, patterns, programming, and imprinting across all time and space, in all dimensions and levels, and all places and planes, that are not in alignment with my highest Akashic blueprint, to leave my body, mind, and energy field now.

Beings of Light, please remove and recycle this energy for the highest good of all.

After clearing out any old energy, it's important to fill yourself up with your own highest and best energy and information because that is one of the ways we stay clear and present. This Prayer to Fill Up With Akashic Energy is a good tool for this:

Please fill me up with the highest and best Akashic Record information and the highest and best physical-level energy and information I can now hold. Thank you for your healing today.

Divine Alignment: The Prayer for Aligning with Your Soul

This prayer can be used daily to remind us that we are divine beings of light and all the abundance of the universe is here for our benefit. Remember, you can use all of these prayers daily inside or outside of the Akashic Records. You may memorize them, and use them often, because they are different than the Akashic Records prayers themselves.

THE PRAYER FOR ALIGNING WITH YOUR SOUL

Spirit, Source, Universe, please show me what it feels like to be the highest, brightest, most expansive and aligned self that I can be today. Please open my heart to know the truth of my divinity and allow me to receive all the good that is within and without. Please guide me on my next steps to being abundant in all ways with ease and grace.

Practicing What You've Learned

Think about somebody you're not feeling comfortable or happy with. Remember, you are still at the beginning of learning an expansive body of work, so I suggest you take it slow with the type of questions you ask. It's very early in the process to ask important questions such as, "Should I end this relationship?" or, "Is this the time to quit my job?" In the beginning, our ego or personality may jump in and answer "Yes!" and you might be unaware that it wasn't the Beings of Light, but instead your ego. A more positive question to ask would be, "How can I be more present in this relationship?" or, "What would be helpful for me to know so that I may bring more peace and harmony to my job?" Remember, we can't change others, and asking specific questions about them is outside of integrity. You can ask, "How am I to smooth and ease the relationship with my boss?"

At this time, let us start with a secondary relationship such as a friend or a coworker. Is there a pattern with this person that repeats itself? An example would be that each time you're told to work on a project together, he or she takes control, or possibly leaves all the work for you to complete. You feel this is a situation that would need to improve for you to stay at your job. You can ask a variety of questions related to how you can create a more harmonious relationship, such as:

✦ Is there something I'm not allowing myself to know about this dynamic?

✦ Is my ego getting in the way?

✦ Is there something blocking me from moving deeper into my heart?

✦ Is denial playing a role in what I need to know about this situation?

✦ Is the Forgiveness Prayer appropriate in this scenario?

Many of the energy patterns people carry were created in their childhood. Most of the time we are completely unaware of these patterns because they are programmed into us by our families, and not by our own doing. These unconscious patterns may push our buttons and trigger an angry or fearful response from us. If you notice this happening to you, do some clearing work on these issues one at a time by asking questions in your Akashic Record. Here are just a few quick and easy questions:

✦ Is the other person's energy in my space?

✦ Am I allowing it?

✦ Will the Prayer for Clearing Others' Energies be effective to release it now?

For this exercise, please contemplate a situation in your life that's not immensely upsetting, but is one in which you have some minor conflict or problem. I highly recommend that you wait until you are more experienced in working in your Akashic Record to dive into significant relationships in your life such as your marriage or your relationship with your parents or siblings. You may find it easier to practice receiving information about a relationship from the past that still hurts, or upsets you whenever you think of it. Maybe it is a relationship with an old friend that you don't see any longer, or an ex-boyfriend or girlfriend. Pick a relationship that has ended but that you feel is unfinished. You may ask questions about that relationship to truly bring it to completion.

Here's a list of question that may be helpful to start with:

+ Did I have karma to complete with that person?
+ If I did, is it complete now, or what else may I know about that karma?
+ Were there soul contracts?
+ Are those contracts complete?
+ What else can I know about this?
+ Is there a better question for me to ask to receive the information I'm looking for?
+ Do I need more information, or is relationship complete? Am I done?

Sometimes there isn't a lot of information, so we can ask:

+ What resources do I have that can assist me in completing this past relationship?

+ How can I feel better about it? How can I release any old guilt to move the memory of it into a place of highest good?

These are all valid and valuable questions to ask. The more specific we can be, the easier it is for our Beings of Light not only to answer us, but also to answer us specifically. I cannot remind you enough how important it is to learn the art of asking questions that can offer you the most specific, action-oriented answers.

Bringing Grace into the Physical: The Energy Release Grace Point

I've given you some powerful and profound healing prayers and tools for you to use immediately, which you can also share with anyone who may need the healing they offer. Now I'm going to offer a more physical aid: a simple, quick-release healing tool called the *Energy Release Point*, also known as the grace point, and it is always as close as your hands. We use this point with our intentions for clearing and releasing energies that are not beneficial to us.

The Energy Release Point uses the naturally occurring energy flow in the human body; this point is in alignment with the acupuncture meridian system, and connects us consciously to our heart. We use this point as a physical anchoring and to direct the energy through our intention and gentle touch. In doing so, we will feel ourselves being supported to bring more grace into our lives. The main point is in the lower left quadrant of your right palm (see the following picture), which is connected to the heart center. The Energy Release Point is found in the soft tissue of the hand, so be gentle on yourself. You just have to touch the point gently; you don't have to dig in deep. You may use either your right hand or left hand. I suggest you ask in your Akashic Record which hand is better for you to use when releasing blocked energy patterns.

By connecting deeply to our hearts through intention and Divine Grace, we are able to clear karma and release limiting conditions, patterns, false beliefs, and past judgments—just to name a few. When you hold the Energy Release Point in combination with the Forgiveness Prayer, you have created a powerful tool to clear karma. You may also open your Akashic Record while holding that point on your palm to connect with your heart, and then ask to receive more clarity and information.

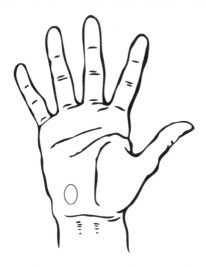

The Energy Release Grace Point. Drawing © Bruno Rendon. Used with permission.

This point connects you directly to your heart center, strengthening your connection in your Akashic Record while opening you to Divine Grace. It also releases contracted energy throughout your body. It can support your focus and insights so that new information is received with more clarity. Once you have fully integrated the new insights into your body, you receive it on a cellular level.

The foundation of this Energy Release Point is unconditional love, which is supported by the divine vibration of the Akashic Records. By connecting consciously, and physically, to our heart through the heart meridian point, we can move into empowerment. We make a conscious choice to clear unwanted and painful emotions and trauma, rather than allowing reactive patterns to rule our lives. When you create an intention based on your desire, you are taking responsibility for the information received and the healing taking place.

I discussed karma earlier as being like an unfinished pie. Another way to look at karma is as an incomplete circle. If you draw a line to create a circle, and you don't finish drawing the whole circle, you've left it incomplete. When we don't complete a cycle, we create karma by jumping out or leaving the circle, leaving something in our lives unfinished. Karma is about concluding what we came to accomplish to complete the circle, or the story. It is always about our soul's growth. It may be something that we wished to learn, or to achieve. Often the best shortcut to bring this karma to completion is through love and forgiveness. That's why forgiveness works to clear karma, leaving you in a place of pure, unconditional love. As we deeply forgive, we move our souls into unconditional Divine love. By activating and accessing the Energy Release Point in our palm, we are doing something very similar. We are opening our hearts, and we are asking through intention to forgive and complete whatever we have left undone.

Consider this: karma can be something we reincarnated to finish from one or more past lives. What you may find in this lifetime is that you meet a person with whom you have karma (an incomplete circle). He might be stuck in an old, angry, aggressive pattern, and if you react to him with anger and aggression, you are not completing the karma. You are just continuing it in the same fashion. If you have an intention to clear the karma so that this pattern can be released, you will see that angry person as a divine soul wearing aggressive patterns of anger. Your intention to complete the karma shifts your energy into one of forgiveness and understanding, so that you are able to separate from the triggering emotions and instead move into a place of grace, caring, and wisdom. Using your Energy Release Point while forgiving this person, and by being in unconditional love, will help you to understand, release, and complete the circle. All of these pieces will complete the old energy, moving you into a place of love and completed karma, and then the issue can evaporate. The good news is either you become friends with that person or you never have to see him again; either way, the outcome can be one of completion.

If a person is particularly unpleasant, you may decide you never want to see her again, or you may find that you have to work through an old energy pattern of which neither you nor she were aware. If you can both work through it together, by recognizing it, understanding it, and learning something from it, then one or both of you can grow past the stuck energy pattern. The old pattern that held the two of you together can transform into a new type of relationship. You will soon discover as you work through these old patterns that all is in Divine order as we continue to grow and expand on our life journey. The Energy Release Point in our palm helps us to complete our karma so that we can move forward and create peace, love, and harmony in this world through our own transformational work.

You can use this powerful grace point either outside or inside of the Akashic Records. Here is a sample of an intention you can use: "I uplift and bring to completion that which no longer serves me," or, "Please help me uplift and bring to completion that which no longer serves me." Another one is, "Uplift and bring this emotion to completion." The Energy Release Point can also be used with healing prayers to clear many types of energy. When something comes up, you might want to hold the grace point, and ask which prayers you can use to clear and release any blocks you are working on. Your Beings of Light may say, "Hold your Energy Release Grace Point and say the Forgiveness Prayer." Both of these tools are going to help clear karma while releasing, uplifting, and bringing the old energy to completion.

If you received profound wisdom, or have, an "aha!" moment, you would again hold your grace point while using this intention: "I want to integrate this wisdom and this information. I want to integrate this knowing and this big-picture view of the world." You can also use that same intention to integrate information even when you're not in the Records. Say you are sitting on the beach watching a beautiful sunset, and you are filled with love and awe of the grandeur of the world around you, and your heart spontaneously opens. Use your grace point here to anchor the feeling into your body on a cellular level. You are anchoring the blessed and blissful feeling, and what is wonderful about using your grace point is that you can immediately remember that feeling at any given moment. When you bring a feeling into your body through your grace point, it never leaves you. All you have to do is hold the grace point with the intention that you're going to relive this feeling of bliss. You're going to bring that feeling back into your body in a tactile way. I love to use my grace point when I see a giggling baby. The baby touches my heart and makes me laugh. For me that's a blissful feeling I want to relive. You can choose whatever feelings bring you joy or bliss.

Clearing Emotions with Emotional Trigger Words

The following is an emotional vocabulary spectrum you can use as a guideline in your Akashic Record whenever you are working on blocked emotional patterns and triggers. To use it, before you open your Record, ask yourself what you are feeling about an issue, using the following words to help trigger your feelings. Then rate each word on the intensity of the emotions it triggers, on a scale from 1 to 10. Then open your Akashic Record and ask your Masters to give you insight into those emotions. Continue to ask questions to gain clarity and reduce the intensity of the emotional trigger word. Write in your journal the original number that you rated yourself, what the Masters told you, and what the final numbers were once you integrated the information. If possible, work through it until you have your "aha!" moment. Your goal is to de-trigger the emotional response to as low an intensity as possible; this may take more than one session in your Record to achieve. Using this emotional scale can help you focus the access to your Record and bring clarity to your questions for your Beings of Light.

Ask your Beings of Light which word to work on to clear any hidden blocks around it. Let them give you a word from the list. If they tell you that your word is *discouragement*, or *insecurity*, or *depression*, you would work with just that word during this process.

This is really a phenomenal process. You can work through a majority of these words to clear or reduce their influence on your trigger points in your life. Try to work with the word until you are down to a 1, 2, or 3 force of intensity. For many of us, all of these emotions often contain powerful charges and blocked energy, so I felt that this effective exercise would help you dislodge hidden energy that could be impeding your spiritual progress without your knowledge. These emotional responses are often well hidden by us until we become triggered and upset by them. Working on them when you are not in an emotionally triggered state can help you defuse a possible volatile situation in the future much quicker, and with harmony and understanding.

Here are some words for you to rate on an emotional intensity scale of 1 through 10 (1 being the lowest):

- ✦ Impatience
- ✦ Overwhelm
- ✦ Disappointment
- ✦ Worry
- ✦ Blame
- ✦ Anger
- ✦ Revenge
- ✦ Hatred
- ✦ Rage
- ✦ Jealousy
- ✦ Judgment
- ✦ Insecurity
- ✦ Guilt
- ✦ Unworthiness
- ✦ Fear
- ✦ Grief
- ✦ Powerlessness
- ✦ Discouragement
- ✦ Depression
- ✦ Frustration
- ✦ Irritation
- ✦ Helplessness
- ✦ Despair
- ✦ Shame

At first you may not recognize when you are triggered, but as you become more experienced, the Beings of Light will guide you to your emotional blocks. As you are learning to go deeper in your Record, start working with this exercise two or three days a week. I can't stress enough how important it is to open your Record consistently in order to work at deeper levels. Just as with any relationship, it takes time to build trust—in this case, your trust for your own ability to receive information.

You can start by opening your Record, and then ask the Beings of Light for a word to work on with their guidance. Then you ask your Beings of Light, "Where in my body do I hold this emotion?" After you receive the answer, just write it down. Then ask, "When was the first time I experienced it in this life?" You might be given an age or a date, and you can ask if there is a story or more information. You could ask, "What will be useful for me to know about this in relation to how this is affecting me? How does it affect me? How does this limit me?" You could ask for specific tools to use to clear it by asking for prayers to uplift and release the emotion, the feeling, or the energy, and don't forget to use your Energy Release Grace Point along with saying the clearing prayers.

An important habit to create from the beginning is to always remember to fill yourself up with the highest and best level of energy and Akashic light when you're finished clearing. This is a great tool to use and practice every day, and it will ensure you don't have any voids in your energy field from the release.

The universe doesn't like voids, so it will fill it. You always want to be the one filling your voids, so use the prayer that was given to you in the Akashic Knowing Wisdom Prayer System.

Releasing Physical Pain

If you don't have any pains or physical issues, I am so happy for you. If you have one or more, such as shoulder aches, hand pain, foot problems, or a bad knee, the Beings of Light can work with you to help clear it. You will go into your Akashic Record to ask, "Is this pain part of my physical body, or is it in my emotional body?" You want to find out the origin of it, so ask your Beings of Light, "What can you tell me about this pain?" Another important question to ask them is, "Is this pain mine or someone else's?" We take on pain from other people for numerous reasons—some people are invasive and a literal "pain in the neck." To go even deeper into the origin of the pain, you can ask, "Is this pain created in present time, or does it come from an earlier period in my life? Is it from five years ago? Is it from childhood? Or is it from a past life?"

It's surprising how many people have pains in their sides, backs, or arms. It's useful to clear the pain out, as something like that typically comes from a past-life wounding. And of course you should ask, "Is there a prayer that I can use to uplift and release this pain?"

Healing Fear

One of the most prevalent triggers we humans have is fear. Some of us have many fears, and others only a few. Either way, fear impedes our abilities to live loving and abundant lives. We are consciously aware of some of our fears, such as a fear of water, needles, dentists, driving, or investing money, to name just a few. Many more fears are unconscious. Did you ever wonder why you might fear having a serious relationship? Are you afraid of being wrong, of not being special, of not being important to someone? Those fears are often driven from the unconscious, leaving us in a constant state of repeating patterns that those fears helped us to form.

Heartache is widespread, and it often has its beginnings in other lifetimes. We come here to Earth to bring it to completion, by repeating a relationship similar to the one that left karma attached to it. For example, in a past life (or even more than one), you were with the love of your life, and then he left you, or he passed away, which left you with a broken heart. So you incarnate into your current life with a broken heart, which is part of finishing that karmic cycle. This reincarnating is then about you healing your broken heart with unconditional love. We heal pain by taking chances, and, where loving another is concerned, that means really loving someone else again. The challenge comes when we have to put ourselves out there, to find someone we can love and who loves us back. For most people, the risk is too great, so they stop themselves from being vulnerable and committed in a loving relationship.

The Energy Release Grace Point and the healing prayers are very useful in clearing a past-life broken heart, karma, and any physical or emotional trauma. We can heal things affecting us in this life that we aren't even aware have an effect on us other than pain (which is quite obvious). For example, I had a client ask for an Akashic Record consultation because he had a fear of water, as in swimming or boating. The Beings of Light showed me a scenario in which the client had drowned in more than one past life. I told him what I had received, and it helped to release the fear. Many of these fears have no roots in our current life; we have the fear but do not know why or remember any trauma. Past-life fears affect us, and we really don't know why. The truth is we are all carrying some of that emotional pain, that kind of emotional scarring from some trauma in another lifetime. We come to this lifetime so that we can heal and clear all of these issues, so we can live fully and love deeply. So if you are afraid of love, or water, or anything else, start working in your Akashic Record to clear your aversion to whatever comes up for you.

Fear of being seen is another leftover issue from past lives. Many of us are afraid to be seen because we were killed in a past life for speaking out in public or for being healers. This is common for people who are involved in the healing arts, such as healers, psychics, intuitives, Akashic Record consultants, channels, and so on. We can clear any of these leftover energies by melding the old energy with the higher vibrational frequency of the Akashic Field of energy. The shift happens when there is a combination of these energies.

When we are in the high-vibration energy of our Akashic Records, we receive information, wisdom, and clarity from our Beings of Light and Teachers. They have given us gifts of sacred prayers and the grace point to raise our frequency to make it easy for us to bring old energies to completion. The Beings of Light have said that one of the reasons we bring these energies forward in this lifetime is because we have a group contract at this time to work together to heal the energy for ourselves, and in doing so, we are also aiding the world in its healing.

As we heal pain, trauma, and heartbreak, as we rebalance the masculine and feminine energies that have been out of balance for thousands and thousands of years, as we do our own personal work again, it goes back to the fact that we truly are all one with Divine Source energy. The healing we do for ourselves ripples out into humanity and we all receive healing. Whichever energies we heal for ourselves, we are also healing for others, because we are all one. We are healing the energy for the world, and we're shifting the energy and the paradigm on planet Earth at this time. It's a great gift that we give to humankind: as we do our own healing work, we are gifting the lifting of that energy across the globe. And, as you do your work, you are also a contributor to this process. Thank you for that.

Take a moment to absorb all that you have accomplished up to this point. In this chapter, you have been guided through a lot of important work. You first learned to open your own Akashic Record just a few chapters ago, and then worked through asking some simple questions, and now you have moved more deeply into your Record. If you feel tired after working through this chapter, treat yourself to a nice warm bath and a cup of tea. If possible, go to bed early, because it is important to take good care of your body. When you are working in the Records, you are placing yourself in a very high vibrational frequency, so when you leave that energy you drop into a lower energy field, which may make your body feel heavy and tired. Also, the release of old energy patterns that you have been holding, often for years or lifetimes, can add to your feeling exhausted. Imagine carrying around a heavy object for hours, and when you put it down, you suddenly feel so much lighter; a weight has been lifted. When you are working in the Akashic Records the weight can be both literal and figurative.

You have moved through quite a bit of Akashic Records teaching up to this point, so let's look back at what you have learned thus far:

+ Akashic Knowing Wisdom Prayer System: Page 79

Remember to continue opening your Record as much as possible. Use the emotional trigger word exercise to help you clear old energies faster. Ask in your Record for healing and guidance to help in organizing your day or week. Most importantly, remember to make a list of questions in your journal that you want to ask each day, and record those answers in your journal. I know once you start working in your Akashic Record, you will love this work and the unconditional love always available to you inside your Record. I hope you are enjoying this work as much as I do.

Chapter 4

The Expansive Akashic Field

30 Questions to Help You Go Deeper into Your Record

In this chapter, we're going to work with more questions to help you go deeper into your Akashic Record. First, though, make sure you're grounded and clear. Take a few minutes to allow your physical body to drop back into your chair. Allow yourself to connect to our dear Mother Earth beneath your feet. Take a couple of deep breaths. Consciously draw all of your scattered energy back right here, right now, into this present moment, into this present time. When you are completely present, ask the assistance of the Beings of Light of the Akashic Field to help you create a sacred space as you go forward, deepening in your Akashic Record, and to help you understand the wisdom that you will receive. Open your mind and your heart, and then ask for their assistance and guidance. Ask for the help from the Beings of Light in receiving information with clarity and with ease. Always give great thanks for all the love and wisdom that you were given here, each and every day.

It is now time to use the **Akashic Knowing Wisdom Prayer System**. Please pick one of the three prayers from Chapter 2 that resonates with you today.

Let us return to your original desires from earlier in the book, when you wrote down what you were looking for in accessing your Akashic Record. For example, say your intention was to be able to access your personal Akashic Record deeply and easily, and to be able to use your Record all the time, every day. You could now go deeper with your questions by asking if there is anything blocking you from receiving more information about your desire. The following is an example of how your Akashic Record session would proceed.

Set your intention, pick which prayer you'll use today, and open your Record. Then work through questions such as these:

+ Is there anything blocking me from accessing my Akashic Record with ease?

✦ Is there a baby step that I could take that would make it easier?

✦ Is there another step that I'm missing in accessing my Akashic Record with ease?

✦ Do I have this ability?

✦ Did this come from my current life?

✦ Did it come from a past life?

✦ Did it come from my childhood?

✦ Is there something else I can know about this?

✦ Is there something that is limiting my view of this desire?

In the following list, I have given you 30 more questions to help you to continue to go deeper in your Record and clarify the information you're receiving. This is how to find information that is truly useful to you, and how to receive a full answer, as I talked about with the maypole dance. You continue asking questions until you feel you truly grasp the information and concepts and can let go of old beliefs and shift your perception to heal yourself. You can combine or reconfigure some of the questions to fit your personal needs. Remember, the more specific your questions are, the greater amount of information you will receive. As I explained in earlier chapters, there is an art to asking questions that yield the greatest amount of information. And as with any skilled artist, you must practice in order to raise and refine your skill levels. As a novice Akashic Records reader, the intention is to build your skill level in opening the Records, and then in receiving information that will help you move your life forward with ease and in the least painful way.

QUESTIONS TO DEEPEN YOUR AKASHIC RECORD WORK

1. Is there another question that I should be asking, or a different way for me to ask it?

2. Are there any blockages or energy that I need to clear related to this issue?

3. Do I need more information on this issue?

4. Is there something I'm not seeing?

5. What is limiting my view of this subject?

6. Am I being influenced by something outside of myself that affects how I see or relate to this subject?

7. Is there a different or easier way to look at this issue?

8. Do I hold a mental view of this subject or situation that does not serve me?

9. Am I holding an expectation of what I think the truth should be in this area or subject? If so, what is it?

10. Is my ego, mind, or emotions blocking me from clearly understanding this information?

11. Is there something I need to do to improve my relationship with others?

12. Is fear blocking me from going deeper in this area or subject? If so, how can I clear it?

13. What information am I ready to know about this issue?

14. Is denial playing a role? If so, how do I move through it?

15. What is my primary issue right now, and how is it blocking my clarity in this area or subject?

16. Is there something or someone I have given my power to in the past, which is having a negative effect on how I see, relate to, or let go of this subject?

17. Who said I couldn't go into this area of life?

18. Is there anything disguised, unknown, or suppressed that I may know now, or that keeps me from knowing what I need to know?

19. How can I handle this issue, problem, or need with greater ease or grace?

20. Why am I afraid of who I will become when I let it go?

21. Is there a belief system or set of ideals that no longer serve me, which stops me from living a happy life?

22. What is my greatest challenge or fear at this time? What is the root of it?

✦ What resources do I have to help me resolve it?

✦ What lessons can I learn from it?

23. What talents did I come to this life with that I might need to use to further my growth, business, or relationship?

24. Are there any relationships that are not working for my highest good?

25. What resource(s) can I use to assist me with parenting and/or marriage?

26. What is the underlying issue in my relationship with my [mother, boss, spouse, etc.]?

27. What do I need to know about this situation? How do I bring this to a favorable resolution?

28. What message would my Beings of Light want me to know at this time?

29. Are there any repeating patterns or behaviors I need to address?

30. Is there a lesson or objective I need to learn or be aware of?

Let's use the example of a couple that is feeling challenged in their relationship. They fight a lot but not about anything in particular. They are both constantly in a bad mood but don't know why. Both people feel unloved and insecure but haven't admitted it to themselves or to their spouse. Imagine this is you, and you decide to work in your Akashic Record to receive information and to bring love and happiness back into the relationship, but you don't know where to start asking questions. You could ask your Beings of Light, "What is the best question for me to ask about this relationship? Would it be helpful to do some forgiveness work in this relationship? What would be helpful for me to know about my soul contract with this person? What other questions can I ask to help me gain clarity?" You can often start with a few questions such as those. The Beings of Light will answer the questions you've asked about soul contracts, and then, to gain clarity, they may suggest Number 4 from the 30 questions, which asks, "Is there something I am not seeing?" The Beings of Light may tell you that the problem is in the way that you speak to your spouse, and that you've moved into judgment where he or she is concerned. As you continue to dialog with your Beings of Light and ask more questions you may find out that it's an old pattern from childhood of low self-esteem that you have not been aware of before. It's causing feelings of insecurity and loneliness. Now your relationship is helping you to become conscious of that pattern so that you can shift and release it. You may have a soul contract to do just that and be supported by your spouse, and once you realize it in your Record, you can do the internal work to remember the truth of who you are as a divine, loving, and loveable soul. As you raise your vibration doing this Akashic Record work, you are also helping to raise the vibration of those around you and to shift the collective energy.

Clearing Childhood Fears

We'll do an exercise now to help you clear some childhood fears that may still be affecting you. The first question to ask is whether there *is* a childhood fear that is affecting your adult life and holding you back. A great second question is to ask when and where you first experienced that fear. You may receive some information about a childhood experience you'd forgotten or are unaware of. You can always ask specific questions, such as, "How old was I?" Then continue to deepen with questions such as, "What other information about this subject could be useful for me to know? What can the Beings of Light share about this fear and how it influences me today?" Just allow yourself to receive whatever information is useful about how this fear is holding you back. The next step is to ask how you can go about releasing this fear. Is there an Akashic prayer that you can use to clear this? If so, which one is it?

In order to deepen into the Record, when you receive one answer you will ask another question either about the answer you received or about another area of the same subject or issue. The next question will take you deeper into the information. Every time you work on a subject you can ask, "What else can you tell me?" or, "Is there more I can know?" or, "Is there something else that's blocking me?" It's always helpful to continuously refer back to the 30 questions I provided you earlier in this chapter.

I recommend you revisit a subject several times. You are growing and learning every time you work in your Record, but remember, we are all a bit like an onion: an onion has many layers to it, and there may be one more layer to peel away. The same is true with your spiritual journey—there is always another layer, or another level of information, understanding, and wisdom. So continue to revisit the same subjects or issues and you will notice that, with time and patience, you'll receive different and deeper answers, which come from releasing layers of energy from the work you did previously on that particular issue.

You might give yourself some time to deepen energetically in your Record before jumping into asking a detailed, multilayered question. I suggest you start with small questions, give yourself time to work in your Record, and build up to the bigger questions. Some of my Akashic Records consultants have noticed that when they were in their client's Record for about 20 minutes, the information started to flow easier. What I have noticed is that when I've been in the Akashic Records for about 15 minutes, the energy intensifies, which allows me to go even deeper and to run a stronger level of Akashic healing energy. When you are deeper in the Records, it is a great time to ask for healing. You can start an Akashic session by asking simple questions such as, "What's the best way to organize my week?" or, "Is there a food that would be particularly beneficial for my body today?" You can just hang out and meditate in the Akashic vibration for 10 minutes or so, maybe do some of your prayers and use the grace point, before you start asking deep questions about big or important subjects.

If you are asking good questions but are not receiving answers, start by writing your questions down. This may get the information flowing because sometimes when we sit and wait and listen we contract and restrict our energy, instead of expanding and allowing the information to come easily. Writing lets the energy flow freely through us because we just write; we are not judging the information. Then you can go back to read what has come through. This process may work particularly well for you in the beginning when your confidence level is building.

What Areas of Life Am I Avoiding?

The next exercise we'll do is to ask is if there is an area in your life you are unwilling to look at. Some people, for example, are unwilling to look at their finances. Others are unwilling to look at their relationships, and still others are unwilling to look at their work. This is another good time to refer to the question list from earlier in this chapter and ask several smaller questions related to the area you don't want to explore. Of course, if you don't want to look at a particular area, you might not even be aware of what that area is. So asking the following questions will help you get started: "Is there an area in my life that I am unwilling to look at? Who or what is keeping me from going into this area in my life?" Once you figure out the area, you can ask questions about it. For example, if you are unwilling to look at your finances, you could ask, "Do I need more information about my finances? Is there something I'm not willing to look at that is limiting my view on my finances? Can you give me more information about why I am unwilling to look at my finances, or, why I am unwilling to look at this area? Is there someone or something that is keeping me from going into this area of my life?" That last one is a key question: "Who or what is keeping me from going into this area? Is it a person, or is it a thing? Is it a collective unconscious belief, or is there actually someone in my life that is blocking me or telling me that I shouldn't bother exploring this area?"

I have noticed that as my students go deeper into exploring their personal issues, they tend to start to access some higher Akashic energies. Again, it's helpful to start out by asking day-to-day questions, such as, "What exercise is best for my body and mind today?" or, "What will bring joy into my life?" At that level, we might find that we are accessing a general group of Beings of Light because the questions are very basic. As we go deeper into multifaceted soul questions, such as, "What did my soul come here to accomplish? What is blocking me from being on my path? What's keeping me from a deeper relationship or a commitment in my life?" often the voices or the energy carry more authority and clarity, with specific instructions and information. Those are the voices that come from the Beings of Light that are deeper in your Akashic Record. You may notice that, when you're asking questions pertaining to different areas within the Akashic Records, other Beings of Light will respond. Their information resonates at different frequencies. The way they explain it to us is there is a hierarchy within everyone's Akashic Record. There are Beings of Light that work with the more mundane and human aspects, ones that are here to guide you on your soul path, ones that work with past lives, and ones that oversee your whole Record, just to name a few areas. We call them the Teachers, Masters, and Lords of the Records, though they are all Beings of Light and Divine Source. You will have the opportunity ask for yourself to whom you are speaking at any given time. That is one way for you to know for sure that you are in the Records, and it isn't your ego giving the information.

The Highest and Best Path Exercise

I am often surprised when my clients and students have judgments about their current path in life. So many of them think they should be doing "something special" to be in alignment with their path. It is as if they think what they're doing isn't of value, or it's a moment in time when they have not found their path, so something must be wrong. The Beings of Light gave me the next process to help you really know that you're on your highest and best path, right now. They want you to drop the judgments about what you are doing. Every journey has a higher purpose, whether it's in the corporate world or the healing world, or whether you are a student or unemployed—you just may not be conscious of what it is yet. They have often told me that if humans knew how revered they are by the Beings of Light, we would stand tall and honor each and every effort we make. They understand the difficulties affiliated with human incarnation. That is why access to the Akashic Records has become more readily available to us at this time. The Beings of Light want to assist us so that we don't have to struggle. They want us to live in joy and love for others and for ourselves.

The following is an excellent process that will help you to realize that you are right where you are supposed to be, doing exactly what you are supposed to be doing. There are several parts to this exercise, so take your time. Don't try to do it all in one sitting. You can ask for help to heal any judgments that you may hold about your blessed path. Remember to use the Forgiveness Prayer in conjunction with this exercise.

We will start with the **Akashic Knowing Wisdom Prayer System**, set our intention for clarity, and then open our Akashic Record using our favorite prayer. This is another opportunity for you to experiment and see what works best for you when communicating with your Beings of Light: you can (a) ask one question, write down the answer, and then move on to the next question, systematically asking one question at a time, or you can (b) read all of the questions in this exercise and ask your Beings of Light to give you the most appropriate information and clearing for you in whatever order is in the highest good for you. It is important to be grateful for the unique soul that you are and enjoy the fun of learning, experimenting, and growing in this process.

Now we'll start the exercise and ask the Beings of Light these questions:

1. Is there information about these judgments I have about my current path that are helpful to know?

2. Are these judgments part of a pattern that can be cleared?

3. Can you help me to clear any judgments I hold about this blessed path?

4. If I am not solidly on my path, can you please guide me back to the center of my path?

5. What do I need to know to redirect my course if I am not fully centered on my path?

It's always a deepening process to add your personal question, or you can ask for support in the following ways:

+ Please guide me back to the center.

+ Are there baby steps I can take to help me move forward?

Please give yourself space and time to integrate the information you receive.

Checking In

If you've been using only one of the Akashic Record prayers throughout this book, take a moment now to check in and ask if you would benefit from using another prayer. I suggest that you ask every day which prayers are useful for your work today. You can ask, "What is the best prayer for me to use for this question?" because there are days when you will find that a different prayer might suit your question better. Checking in with your Beings of Light for the highest and best healing prayers to use today is a great practice to have.

Please make sure that you are documenting in your journal all of the information that you are receiving. Presuming you are keeping a journal, you might jot down those questions at the top of the page tonight, so you will remember to ask, "What is the best prayer for me to use for this question?" before you just pick a prayer out of habit. You can ask in the energy of divine guidance outside of your Record, "What is the highest and best prayer for me to use today for the work I'm doing?"

Gathering Wisdom from Past Lives Exercise

In the next exercise, we will begin to work with past-life information to support you on your path in this present time. We are infinite beings, and most of you have lived at least 500 earthly lives! Imagine all the success you've created in these lifetimes. You've been an entrepreneur, an artist, a scholar, a healer, a warrior, a prophet, an acupuncturist, a monk, and a teacher, not to mention a great parent and a loving spouse. You can reclaim wisdom and know-how from these lives and any other things you are interested in exploring.

I used this exercise when I was writing this book. My first thought when the Akashic Masters told me to bring this Akashic wisdom out into the world by writing was, *I don't know how to write a book!* But my second thought was, *That information has to be in the Akashic Records.* I set about doing the Gathering Wisdom from Past Lives exercise (given at the end of this section) numerous times with the intention to reclaim past-life information, energy, and wisdom from a life when I was a "Successful Published Author." I also reclaimed lifetimes in which I wrote with ease. It's very helpful to think of and ask about different aspects of what you want to reclaim. If you notice, I didn't just say "Author"; I requested information from lives in which I was *successful* and *published*. I may have lives in which I was a starving author or maybe a poor writer, and I don't desire to reclaim that information.

Let's get started with this process for you. Decide what it is you wish to reclaim that will be helpful for you in your life now. It is often best to write out your questions first, so let's try that now by thinking of four to six questions you can ask about reclaiming past-life wisdom that's important to you. Next you start with the **Akashic Knowing Wisdom Prayer**

System. When your Record is open, you will start asking the questions you've written out. A great question to add is, "Please show me a past life when I was on my path with clarity, trust, and power in the Light." Ask your Beings of Light to tell you about these lifetimes. Then ask, "Is there anything blocking my ability to reclaim the information from a lifetime?" When we clear blocks in this lifetime or another, it is useful to reclaim the higher vibration from the past life when you walked in the light because that was a powerful time for you. You'll want to clear anything that keeps you from accessing and reclaiming that past-life information.

The next part of the question is to find out if there is anything you can release that is masked, hidden, or cloaked. In asking the question in that way, you open up the opportunity for more information to come through. Sometimes when we ask a general question such as, "Is there anything blocking me from reclaiming this?" we receive no response or very little information. But when you ask the question, "Is there anything masked, hidden, or cloaked?" things that are veiled may become visible. Think of your questions as being an energy vibration. When you ask unspecific questions the energy link is weak; in comparison, a specific and well-thought-out question or series of questions carries a vibration that expresses your deep desire and strong intention to go into the depth of this information. Then, you are allowed to see behind the curtain. Use this question to go deeper: "Is there anything masked, hidden, or cloaked that I can release right now to help bring this information more fully into my mind, body, and soul?" Ask the Beings of Light, "Please help me to release whatever it may be, and share with me that information which is useful in my soul's growth." At the end of this process you may include a visualization meditation to reclaim more of the high-vibrational past-life energy and wisdom.

Often, well-articulated, specific past-life questions can be enlightening and fascinating because, at times, we think that a past life in which we were fully on our path was a magical or mystical kind of life. Yet I've seen many times when those lives were simple, or we even lived in what we consider today as poverty. Often, I have seen lifetimes when the soul was severely challenged, yet that soul lived a profound life of service filled with love and light. So do not be surprised by what you are shown of your past life or lives when your path was dedicated to love and light.

Some of the most fascinating work and clearing we can do is when we start to look at our past lives that have had different paths or purposes. I like to ask the Beings of Light to "share with me lifetimes in which I was Enlightened or Awake." The information I've received from this question has often astounded me, because I was expecting to hear that I was a powerful and just king, or an oracle goddess, or some great Light guru or prophet, but it was often quite the opposite. So explore some of these topics for yourself and discover who you truly are.

Here's an example of this exercise that one of my students shared on an Akashic Study Group call:

Jen: The first picture they showed me was of a hermit walking alone, and I felt resistance as I found myself thinking, "No, I don't want to see that." They then showed me a woman. She was in a room; she had a lot of large instruments—a telescope and a globe. I got a sense of myself in the room reading, writing, creating, and living in a beautiful state of feeling. In that life, I was just following my instincts by doing these scientific experiments, which I so enjoyed. I also shared my wisdom and abundance. I had a staircase to the stars. It felt like I was communicating with different beings on different levels of consciousness, and I laughed. I was present on all levels. It felt really good. Interestingly, as I was asking if anything was blocking me, I got a sense of standing in a doorway. It was smoky, and then a woman came through the smoke with a cheese sandwich!

Lisa: [laughing]

Jen: Funny, right? That was kind of funny. I was like, "What the heck?!"

Lisa: They do have a sense of humor.

Jen: Yeah! But you know, I think I worry too much about small things like where my next meal is coming from. They told me that what is blocking me is like a piece of a puzzle. I have to gather my sense of adventure, and trust my work, as it is my part of the puzzle.

Lisa: You could also continue to ask more questions such as, "Where is this lifetime taking place? Is this a place on Earth? Is this a real lifetime? Can you give me the year, or a date?" You certainly don't have to ask all these questions, but sometimes it's fun to ask so you can go deeper into the information.

We can always ask more questions if we're unsure. Sometimes it's interesting to say, "Is this a specific lifetime I lived? Or is this a conglomeration of lifetimes or symbolic of something in particular? Is this more of a state of being than a time and place?" You can just go deeper and deeper with those questions. Often, my students will receive information on many different past lives. I wish to remind you that you don't have to figure out the locations or the time period, you simply need to ask the Beings of Light, "When? Where?" By doing so, you will usually be given a clear and concise date, such as, "It's the 1400s," or, "It's 3000 BC in Spain."

In the Course 2 workshop, we delve deeply into understanding our soul lineage, which is connected to our soul purpose in this life. As we explore more deeply who we have been in other lives, we realize why we came to this lifetime. Here's another example from one of my students who asked for information about a lifetime in which she was in alignment with her soul purpose and path:

Sally:I had what felt to be a very simple and very peaceful lifetime in which I was doing a lot of work with Mother Earth and with water. I found myself standing in the moonlight in front of the water doing a very sacred ceremony with the water and the earth. It felt wonderful; very sacred. When I asked if there is anything blocking me or masked, hidden, or cloaked, I received information that I have blocked myself. My personality now does not allow me to feel my self-worth. Also, more importantly, they told me that I had made a vow in that lifetime to that sacred place, which doesn't exist any longer. This has left a part of me stuck in that other time, place, and dimension. This is all very interesting to me and I know I have more information and clearing to receive.

Lisa: Thank you, and of course there's always plenty of time to keep working on those lifetimes. It is fascinating that you made a vow to protect that place, and it no longer exists. So how do you reclaim that energy, or the wisdom? We ask the Beings of Light, "How can I reclaim this? Is there a healing prayer that I can use? Is there a tool that I already have in my tool kit to help reclaim the energy? Can you help me to reclaim that energy?"

Now it's time to do the visualization to assist in reclaiming past-life energy. As you do this meditation, you will be led back into the past life of your intention, and as you come back up the road, in the meditation, you will be literally bringing past-life energy and wisdom into this space-time continuum with you. Many of you will feel this in your bodies. What often happens for my students and clients is that just by witnessing the lifetime and acknowledging their experience they are unlocking the stuck energy. When mixed with the high and divine vibration of the Akashic Field, they are aided in reclaiming that energy and the information they desire.

To prepare for this meditation, please allow yourself to sit back in your chair and relax. You can soften your eyes as you read. The intention you will be setting for this meditation is to reclaim the information, wisdom, power, and healing abilities from other lifetimes. Ask the Beings of Light, "Please help me to reclaim everything that is useful and helpful for me in this area of my life right now." It is a simple intention. You are asking for help to reclaim the highest and best good that you are ready to integrate into your life.

GATHERING WISDOM FROM
PAST LIVES EXERCISE

Take a few deep breaths, being sure to breathe deep into your whole physical body, from the top of your head to the tips of your toes. As you breathe deeply, imagine that it's a beautiful spring day and you're walking down a country road, and, as you walk down this road you see a forest ahead. As you slowly walk towards that forest, you know that you're stepping slowly back in time. With every step you take you go another step back in time. You've reach the edge of the forest. You peer through the trees and step onto a narrow path. It's a beautiful path, padded with leaves and moss, and though it's not very bright under the trees, it feels very safe. It's a warm day, and it feels luscious and cool as you walk deep into these woods.

As you walk down the path, continuing back in time, you look to your left and you see some lights deep in the forest. You look off to your right, and there are more lights sparkling through the trees. You see some dense patches of woods, and then here and there between the trees you see sparkling lights. Some look like lamplights, some look like campfire lights.

You continue to walk farther down this road. As you walk through the forest, you're walking past many, many, many past lives that you've experienced; just continue looking off to the left and then off to the right. You've seen these lives; you've seen these lights. You're feeling secure, and as you continue to walk you see a village's lights sparkling out in the distance. You may hear some singing or laughter out in the forest. These are all past times in which you've lived. You may hear the families you've had. You see them, you feel them, you know they're out there.

You've been to this forest, deep, deep into the past. You feel called to visit one of these past lives. So you turn toward the lights of your choosing, or toward some singing; toward a building or a village or some laughter. Something catches your attention so you go deeper into the woods, feeling that you're safe, feeling that you are always guided, guarded, and protected on these journeys.

As you walk into a clearing, a lifetime unfolds in front of you. Experience this lifetime—it's a wonderful lifetime that answers your intention. It may have been filled with friends and family, or it may have been very solitary life. Take in the experience this life offers you. Ask the Beings of Light and Akashic Teachers to bring you the wisdom and gifts of this lifetime. Those gifts may come to you from the people as they sing to you, feed you a wonderful feast, or hold you in their arms. Merge with Mother Nature, bathe in a stream, or climb a mountain to receive your gift. Whichever way they come to you is just perfect, so receive your gifts with gratitude.

Breathing deeply while holding your grace point, ask for assistance to grace in this wisdom, this light, this knowing, this love; gracing it deeply into your physical being. You feel all of the light and love and wisdom. Thank those who have given gifts and love to you. You may hug and kiss the people you remember as you say goodbye.

As you head back to the main road, back to the main trail, breathe deeply and continue to hold that grace point as you continue to grace and ground this wisdom into your body in this present moment.

Step onto the path home. Head back up the path through the forest, back through time, heading home into this present moment, into this present time. As you walk up the road, still seeing the lights and the trees, with song and laughter in the distance, you know there are many, many beautiful lifetimes that you've had and you are always welcome to go back to them, to experience them, to claim that wisdom, that love, that knowledge.

Right now, you see the sunshine as the forest ends, and the main road appears ahead of you. You come out of the deep forest, into the light in the fields, breathing deeply, right back here and now, in this present moment.

And as you come back to the present, just allow yourself to feel your feet planted on the floor right here in your room and notice your physical body sitting here in your chair. Tap your feet gently. Breathe deeply and open your eyes. Give thanks for the great gifts that you've been given. Welcome home.

To listen to the recorded version of this meditation, please visit *www.theinfinitewisdom.com/past-life-wisdom*. You can listen to the recording as often as you'd like, to continue to go back and reclaim different energies and different past lives' wisdom.

I love hearing all about the experiences my students have when doing this meditation. Some of them mention how the Beings of Light remind them of the simplicity, the higher truth, the family connections, and the expanse we are all part of in this life. Their work with us is to encourage us to be in our hearts with ourselves, whether we are alone or with family and friends. Our higher purpose is to achieve love and compassion for others and for ourselves. Students also say that as they come out of the meditation, the *now* feels like the new earth. They feel themselves moving forward to create with simplicity and grace, and to expand into re-creating some of these beautiful communities that we experience as we travel back into these empowered lives. Often, as I lead a class, the Beings of Light point out that we as souls are all here to reclaim the wisdom that is ours as we go forward to create the life our heart's and soul's desire, a world living in love. We truly are ancient, wise, and infinite souls who have come here, at this time in history, to create heaven on Earth, a new world that resonates at a higher frequency of unconditional love and peace. It takes all of you raising your vibration to raise the vibration of humanity. You may notice there is more love and laughter, with more space to just *be*, with simplicity and grace, as we are moving out of the third dimension, surrounded by so much chatter, and overstimulation with cell phones, computers, texting, and Internet businesses that never close.

We are being guided to tune into our inner knowing through our personal Akashic Record.

Is My Life Preordained?

The Akashic Beings of Light tell us that nothing in this life—or any lifetime, here on Earth or in another dimension—is written in stone. Our souls particularly love coming to Earth because we enjoy free will. We love the process of growth through experience. It may appear as a conflict or struggle in our lives but we have often "written" it into our soul's plan to create the possibility of growth and learning in a specific area. The Beings of Light want to remind us that at any moment, it is possible to awaken and know the truth of who we are as divine souls, in union with Source. Just by knowing "I am a divine being" you raise your vibration, which helps to lift you out of the negative energy of struggle or fear. By opening your Akashic Record, you are consciously moving into the vibration of Source, the highest vibration available. This is why working in your Record is so transformational: you raise your vibration and remember the Divine truth of who you are, as you receive information that helps the ego/personality/mind to understand the issue from a higher point of view.

To this point, I have given you a series of questions to help when you are struggling with conflict or simply one of life's difficulties. If there is something in your life that is making you unhappy, know that you are not alone, as it certainly happens to all of us at one time or another. We think, "What the heck?! Why is this situation in my life? I'm doing my work! I'm trying to stay on my path, to be a good person! And still so many things are not working out very well!" The next process is good to do when you're struggling, or have conflict or recurring situations or issues. As with the other questions and processes I've given you in this book, you can use them in different situations. This process will help you dig a little deeper into what is going on in the background of the circumstance. These questions are broad, yet specific enough to help you receive pertinent information:

+ Is there a preordained arrangement in this situation? In other words, do I have karma to be resolved? A lesson to be learned? A wound to be healed?

+ Am I missing something, or not remembering what is needed in this situation?

+ What am I unaware of?

Let's practice using the preceding questions. Think of a recent issue in your life (I'm praying that everyone's life is issue-free, but, as many of us have noticed, there's usually something going on we'd like to resolve). Maybe your car just broke down, and you have to buy a new one. Or maybe your main relationship is not always ideal. Possibly, you're struggling with your kids' attitude problems. Or you would like a new job because your boss is not treating you well or you were overlooked for a promotion. Whatever it might be at this moment for you, ask in your Akashic Record, "Did I make a vow in a past life that is connected to this situation or pattern? How am I following up on a vow? Is there something about this issue that I've come to work through with this person, or at this job? Is there some karma I have come here to finish that is playing out in this situation? Is there karma to be resolved, a lesson to be learned, a wound to be healed, something for me to learn that I'm unaware of as I'm looking at these circumstances?"

Sometimes, when we have a situation with our boss, we might think that he isn't so bright or so nice, but the truth may be that you came to learn something from him about yourself, or to finish some karma, or to complete a vow. Not always, but often, people come into our lives for a reason. Your responsibility is to find out what that reason is. What are the details of this prearranged matter? Is it a soul contract? What is written into this contract? Is it one of completion, growth, or support? Then the second part of the process is to answer the following questions: "What is it that I'm contributing through my egoistic attitude or my personality? What part of me is adding to this conflict or this suffering?" This is an advanced exercise, so be sure to take the time to reflect on your answers. And always use your journal to write down the questions you ask and the answers you receive.

This type of questioning can really shift our view of the world. When we start to ask questions like, "What role do I play in this conflict? What part of this am I responsible for?" we begin to confront the things we've created in those situations, whether in this present moment or in another life. You'll notice that when you find yourself in a difficult situation, or struggling with an issue, if you just open your Akashic Record to ask some of these questions you will be opening yourself to make big changes and shift in your life and viewpoint. Try these questions: "How can I heal from this situation? How can I let it go with ease and grace? Is there something masked or cloaked that is keeping me from releasing it?"

One of the greatest gifts that we receive from working in the Akashic Records is the ability to see the big picture and have moments of realization that all is not as it first seems with many situations. And with the aid of your own Akashic Record, you can always choose to go deeper. By seeking the hidden reasons, we can find answers that will help us not only at that moment, but in the long term as well. There is no more special a moment than the one you receive from finding your own truth and source of deep love and reverence for your path in this lifetime. The Beings of Light of the Akashic Records are always there ready to serve you in a most meaningful and profound experience. All you have to do is...ask!

Next Steps on Your Akashic Path

I hope you've enjoyed your time learning about your Akashic Record, and that you've found your first steps into your Record to be helpful and enlightening. Your Beings of Light want nothing more than for you to feel their love and for you to have a lifetime filled with everything that's in your highest and best good.

I would encourage you to continue the work you've started here by opening your Akashic Record regularly, if not daily. As we talked about earlier, learning about the Akashic Records is like learning how to read when you were in first and second grade. Chances are that you learned how to read pretty well, but it's not just the act of reading that was so exciting; reading is all about the information you suddenly have access to when you learn how. With the Akashic Records, it's about deepening into the Records and practicing so you have access to more information, knowledge, and wisdom.

This book is only an introduction to the Akashic Records. It would be challenging and a disservice to you if I tried to teach you everything I've learned about the Akashic Records in one book. You would become overwhelmed and most of the information would never be integrated. As with any process of personal growth and spiritual healings, it takes time to understand the layers and depth our self-knowledge exists on. Each level has an inner defense system ready, willing, and able to protect it. That is why some energies continue to carry over, lifetime after lifetime. I highly recommend you take your time in exploring and releasing that which no longer serves your highest and best self. Be reassured that the

Beings of Light will guide you lovingly so as not to give you more than you can handle.

Index

lifetimes, emotional pain
and different, 123-124

lineage,
  galactic or ancient, 77
  Isis, 96
  Osiris, 96

locking your records,
  importance of, 92-93

love, Beings of Light and
  the journey to, 56

meditation,
  energy, 114-116
  Golden Egg, 59
  kite, 61

money nightmares, 39-43

name, opening the
  Akashic Records with
  your, 66

negative energy
  patterns, 21

negative karma,
  releasing, 24

Orion planetary system, 95

Osiris lineage, 96

pain, healing, 148

passive-aggressive
  behaviors, 47

past lives exercise, 165-172

past lives, 20

past-life
  energy, reclaiming, 171
  memories, 91-92
  vows, 21-22, 43
  wisdom, 166-172
  wound, 44

physical clearing, prayer
  for, 125-126

physical pain, releasing,
  145-146

planetary systems,
  prayers to the, 95

Pleiades planetary
  system, 95

Pleiades, 99

Prayer
  for Aligning With
    Your Soul, 131-132
  for Clearing Entities
    and Energy Patterns,
    130-131
  for Clearing Others'
    Energies, 126-127

prayer lineages, 94-101

prayers,
  Akashic, 73-76

Links for Free Downloads

Free Meditation, Questions Answered, and Aura Photographs

Meditation

Download the free guided visualization to help you reconnect with wisdom from your past lives. You can listen to the recording as often as you'd like. You will reclaim different energies and different past lives' wisdom each time you return.

To listen to the recorded version of this meditation, please visit TheInfiniteWisdom.com/past-life-wisdom.

Your Questions Answered

For a helpful Q&A session with some commonly asked questions about the Akashic Records, please visit TheInfiniteWisdom.com/questions-answered.

Aura Photos

One day, to verify the shift in energy my students and I were experiencing when we opened our Akashic Records, we had some aura photos taken. The aura photographs are a wonderful confirmation of the energy changes when we moved from our "normal" state into the Akashic Field using sacred vibrational keys. To see the photos from a variety of teachers, please visit TheInfiniteWisdom.com/auraphotos.

About the Author

With support from the Akashic Beings of Light, **Lisa Barnett** founded the Akashic Knowing School of Wisdom to teach the six new Akashic access prayers she was given by her Beings of Light to create Akashic access with ease and to assist with ascension for humanity. Through her school courses and consultations, Lisa has helped thousands of people around the globe find greater happiness, abundance, and health by accessing their own Akashic Record. As a result, her students and clients have aligned with their souls' paths, learned of their soul contracts, and broken free from limiting vows.

As an internationally respected Akashic Record Master, Guide, and Transformational Teacher, Lisa has more than 20 years' experience guiding people to energetic healing and higher wisdom. She uses her dynamic and powerful shortcuts for accessing the Akashic Record to facilitate the healing of emotional scars and the clearing of soul contracts, and to help people walk their own true path. Lisa lives in the San Francisco Bay Area with her husband and teenage twin daughters.